LIFE
AS SPORT

LIFE
AS SPORT

*WHAT TOP ATHLETES CAN TEACH YOU
ABOUT HOW TO WIN IN LIFE*

JONATHAN FADER

DA CAPO PRESS
A Member of the Perseus Books Group

Editorial production by Lori Hobkirk at the Book Factory
Design by Cynthia Young. Set in 11.75 Adobe Garamond.

Library of Congress Control Number: 2016932027
First Da Capo Press edition 2016
ISBN: 978-0-7382-1895-3 (hardcover)
ISBN: 978-0-7382-1896-0 (e-book)

Published by Da Capo Press
A Member of the Perseus Books Group
www.dacapopress.com

10 9 8 7 6 5 4 3 2 1

For my mother and father, Liz and Jeff . . .
with gratitude for teaching me how to play.

And

for Rosa, Frankie, Nati, and Lucky,
for playing with me every day.

CONTENTS

FOREWORD BY
SANDY ALDERSON

I'm fortunate to be familiar with Jonathan Fader through the great work he does with elite athletes and high achievers in a variety of disciplines. Thus, I was looking forward to learning more about how the strategies he uses can be adapted to everyday life outside the stadium.

I wasn't disappointed.

Right away, I could see that Jonathan has neatly defined a problem so many of us have—focusing on outcomes vs. processes—and encapsulated a method for anybody to solve that problem.

Getting preoccupied with outcomes has certainly been a hazard in all the years I've been in baseball, just as it was when I was in the military and when I made my way through Harvard Law School. How do you acknowledge that outcome pressure exists but identify and establish a process that lets you manage the competing forces in your mind and in your life so that you can make sound, mindful decisions and keep potential consequences in the proper perspective?

Jonathan shows you how in *Life as Sport*.

I was particularly struck by the way Jonathan describes how to identify what motivates you, and how truly important the mental and emotional components of performance really are. It was fascinating to read and learn how my motivation both informs how I approach situations and the techniques I should use in the moment.

In my career as a sports executive, I've always believed that the more you can do to enhance your mental and emotional approach, the more control you'll have and the better your chances for achieving peak performance. It has manifested itself in how I view coaches. I've never chosen one that has been strictly oriented toward mechanical techniques. Rather, I have always preferred coaches who understand how important a strong mental approach is for professional athletes.

Jonathan's insight on that subject reinforced and expanded what I believe about the relationship between the mind, emotions and attitude—and the relationship between attitude and performance. *Life as Sport* gives you concrete ways to build strategies and routines that make the day-to-day process of living life easier, and more enjoyable.

The techniques that he describes (like visualization and adaptive self-talk) are ones that I have tried to use over the years, but struggled with in stressful situations—such as watching an extremely important game come down to the last inning. What Jonathan is able to do in *Life as Sport* is show you how to prepare for success but also how to prepare for times of adversity and high emotion—how to use these skills at the times when you need them the most. It isn't so much about solving a specific problem as it is about maintaining the perspective and emotional balance to be able to approach any situation—positive or negative—with your strongest decision-making powers.

This gives you the freedom to enjoy the moment as it happens, because you're ready for it—and you're not consumed by what has happened in the past or what might happen if you succeed or fail. You will learn how to focus on enjoying the process and by doing so, you are likely to succeed more often.

The tools Jonathan describes are as powerful as any of the statistical or other innovations I've seen in my almost forty years in baseball. Give them, and *Life as Sport*, a try. You won't be disappointed!

Sandy Alderson
New York, NY
January 2016

Success is no accident. It is hard work, perseverance, learning, studying, sacrifice, and most of all, love of what you are doing or are learning to do."

—PELE

INTRODUCTION:
THE GAME OF LIFE

It's your big moment.

You have an important presentation to make. You're getting ready for a big date. Or you have a critical parenting decision to make. You need to be at your best, and you're hoping your best abilities—and judgment—will be there.

There's nothing wrong with hoping to do well. But hoping is not a strategy. The most successful elite athletes have figured out that wishing and hoping aren't going to separate them from the rest of the pack.

They follow a distinct philosophy and set of learnable mental skills that let them prepare more effectively and perform with more focus and freedom.

In *Life as Sport* you will learn that philosophy and the tools to implement it. You'll learn how to *expect* success in your life, not just hope for it.

OVER THE COURSE of a decade, as a sport psychologist for professional teams and world-class athletes, I've been involved in plenty of casual conversations with friends and acquaintances who have a very natural curiosity about the work

I do—both from my perspective as a doctor and the athlete's perspective as a competitor.

They want to know how athletes think and how we work together to improve the way they think. Many times what people are really asking me is, "How different are elite athletes from the rest of us?" And, indirectly, "Is there some kind of trick or shortcut I can take out of their experience to help me perform better in my life?"

I can certainly understand the fascination people have with elite performers. I can't imagine a more interesting profession than working with and getting to know world-class athletes and top-level financial and entrepreneurial executives on a day-to-day basis as a performance coach.

I'm truly fortunate to have the job I have.

Still, many of those casual conversations got to be pretty uncomfortable for me. I felt my own internal pressure to come up with a way to simply and quickly explain the world of performance psychology and share some interesting stories from my career—but without violating the sacred confidentiality promise that governs these professional relationships.

Over time I got better and better at explaining this world of mental coaching—and more importantly I was able to clarify both the specifics of what I do for elite performers and why that work is so enjoyable for me.

The theories and techniques in this book are the result.

Life as Sport is the product of thousands of hours of conversations with athletes from various teams and sports: power forwards, tennis phenoms, power-hitting outfielders, raw minor league prospects, battle-scarred linebackers, journeyman utility players, fading superstar pitchers, hedge fund managers, precocious entrepreneurs, A-list actors, and dozens of other elite achievers in sports business and performing arts.

Each chapter is a compendium of stories, theories, and techniques that have been helpful to players, coaches, and executives in professional sports. I know they work, not only because I've personally witnessed others improve by using them or because they are largely backed by science but because these techniques and this way of being have also been helpful to me.

One important concept that emerged during these casual "cocktail party" conversations was that more than just a set of sport psychology techniques, there was a certain life philosophy that successful athletes lived by: an internal code that allowed individuals with immense talent to reach the highest plateaus of human performance.

Of course, having world-class talent is an important part of achieving those levels of athletic attainment. But many of the identifiable mental characteristics that separate the best from the rest are mental *skills*, not something innate, like height or the ability to turn on a 98-mile-per-hour fastball.

In other words, they're strategies that can be studied, learned, practiced, and improved.

In this book we're going to talk about those skills and what virtually any person can do to improve them—not just to increase performance but also to enjoy the ride.

What do these elite achievers do?

I describe it as a balanced combination of playfulness, reality-based optimism, and a well-honed ability to focus on the present moment.

Take this example of one of my baseball clients, a pitcher I worked with all through his minor league career. When he got the call to the big leagues for his first start, I watched very carefully—hoping he would be able to display the skills I knew he had. As much as I want a positive result for all the clients I work with in sports and other areas, when I watch a performance, I am mostly looking for how my clients perform in terms of their mental game. Do they appear to be focused, centered on each moment? How relaxed are they? What does their breathing look like? Are they able to reset and adjust to a negative outcome? Do they seem confident and aggressive? And perhaps most importantly, do they seem to be enjoying themselves behind their game face?

From the first inning, he looked like he belonged on a major league roster. As he threw each pitch, he seemed to be fully confident about where it was going to end up. When one of the infielders made an error behind him—something that can derail the composure of even the most elite pitchers from time to time—he shrugged it off as something outside of his control and moved on.

Over the course of a few innings he got some tough calls from the home plate umpire, common in the sometimes near hazing of rookie pitchers in the big leagues, and he started to hear it from opposing fans behind home plate. But he seemed impervious to those distractions, and he moved through the opposing lineup once and then again. He kept his head high and his chest out, showing confidence the way we had discussed, and he kept pounding the strike zone.

It looked like it was just him and the catcher out there. It was a very sophisticated game of catch in which the hitter and, thus all pressure and self-evaluation, simply disappeared.

Later I heard some of the coaches and other players talking about him, about how he had such a mound presence out there. He had the composure of a veteran—one of the highest compliments you can pay a newly minted ballplayer.

When you watch a performance as a fan, it's natural to assume that many of the characteristics that make up the player doing his achievements are innate. The guy out there is a natural—a physical and mental marvel—doing things most people couldn't dream of replicating. But that perspective short-changes just how much work goes into achieving at that level. Sure, many professional athletes were born with physical advantages. But to get to the top and stay there, athletes have to go through a tremendous amount of mental training and practice.

I had known this pitcher throughout his time in the minors. He first contacted me as a raw ball of talent, freaked out about the prospect of going to play professionally, thousands of miles from home. Over the years we worked on his mental state as a thing he could practice—just like he would with the slider he was learning. We developed a plan to improve his breathing and gave him a strategy to avoid rushing his delivery—a natural response to the uncomfortable pressure that comes when you think the whole world is watching and waiting for you to pitch.

With some breathing drills—which we're going to talk about in Chapter 4—he was able to relax on the mound and let his talent take over. He was able to quiet his mind and control the relaxation process, leveraging everything in his control to increase his chances of staying positive.

Positivity is a fascinating thing in that most people know at a basic level that being positive is more productive than being negative. But when things start to go wrong, it's easy to lose the commitment to that positive outlook and fall into a spiral where you become focused on things you can't control.

When this happens someplace like on a major league pitcher's mound, it's easy to see the result.

When a pitcher gives up a couple of hits in a row, what he does next sends some powerful signals to both himself and the opposing team. Many times a pitcher in that situation will curse himself and kick the dirt in obvious frustration.

This is an understandable reaction, but it hurts the pitcher on two fronts. First, it adds emotion and stress to the situation, basically guaranteeing that the next few pitches won't be the pitcher's best. Also, it offers powerful positive reinforcement to the opposing batter. He sees the pitcher on the ropes and gains his own confidence.

Over the years we developed a strict system as to what he would do if there was the slightest unwanted outcome or hiccup to his performance. He would get off the mound and enact a few ritualized behaviors to "flush" this outcome and move on. By smoothing some dirt with his foot, raising his head to eye level and pushing out his chest, he was telling his body and the world, "I'm ready to compete."

The philosophy elite performers adopt to achieve this state—and the skills they use—aren't secret, but it's certainly information that is closely protected. An athlete's physical makeup—the attributes of his or her body and the raw power or raw skill used within each sport—is easy to measure and pretty straightforward to train and repair. But mental makeup and "toughness" is harder to quantify, and historically it hasn't been as well understood.

Many competitors over the years have operated in fear that whatever hold they may have on those nonspecific concepts like "confidence" or "the zone" would appear or disappear arbitrarily or at a whim.

But over the last ten or fifteen years athletes have developed more of both acceptance and understanding of mental performance training, and they've been able to work with professionals like myself to hone those skills to the ultimate in competitive sharpness. In this book, you'll get an inside look at the emerging field of "Mental Conditioning."

As you'll see in *Life as Sport*, those skills aren't only useful for raising a hitter's batting average or aiding a pitcher in throwing more strikes; this book will show you how you can use the techniques of sport psychology and the attitudes of the world's top performers to improve your most important performances in life—to really treat your job, relationships, business, and other important activities as sports. In other words, you improve your daily experience by treating life as a game that, with careful thought and science-based technique, can be understood more completely, practiced, and more fully enjoyed.

Every life has its unique challenges. Now each of those challenges will be an occasion to enter the arena—an opportunity to channel your skills, refocus your energy away from the past, and connect in an immediate way with the moment at hand. You'll begin to focus on enjoying the actual process of learning and improvement—not just some arbitrary definition of "achievement" at the end of the process.

And to me that enjoyment is really one of life's most important pieces. When you learn to enjoy the journey—the process of learning and improving—you're providing the fuel for that "mental toughness" you hear athletes talk about all the time. Determination and grit and the ability to "grind it out" are great, but you can't sustain any of that without a source of enjoyment. When you embrace and enjoy the process, you're going to be more satisfied, which makes you more likely to keep up the fight—to "grind it out" when necessary.

CONCLUDE THIS Introduction on a personal biographical note, as writing this book has been a part of both a professional and personal journey for me.

My first professional experience in the world of sport psychology came in 2007 when I began to contribute to Major League Baseball's rookie career development program, an off-season conference for the game's most promising minor league prospects, where they learn how to clear the mental, emotional, and financial hurdles that come when you get to the big leagues. I worked with many star baseball players from a variety of teams in those first couple of years. In addition, this work led me to work with athletes in other sports. Many of the examples in this book are based in part on those early experiences, getting to know the best of the best as they made their way onto the world's stage. I have continued to participate in the MLB rookie program over the past decade and have had many learning experiences while my colleagues and I have worked to help the best and brightest make their entrance into the "Show." In 2008 I started working with the New York Mets as a psychologist for their minor league system under my mentor, Dr. Jeff Foote, who was the sport psychologist for the big league team. In 2014 I moved up to become the Mets' team psychologist, and I now spend a majority of my time working with either the Mets players or elite athletes and performers in other sports and business.

It didn't take long into my work with baseball players to notice that I was referencing techniques and using sports-related anecdotes to teach many lessons outside the world of sports, both to clients in other fields like finance and for mental improvement in other aspects of life like relationships and parenting. Nonsports clients also started asking me for more stories and help in applying the same sport psychology techniques I use with elite athletes to effect change in their lives. I began to adapt all the ideas we've been talking about into understandable and easy-to-learn concepts and techniques for people to apply to many, if not all, life situations—and created the foundation for this book.

Before long I began to think of this philosophy as one in which life's moments were a string of performances—whether you're an athlete or not. Talk to Adrian Grenier about his life as an actor, director, and musician, and you'll hear the *Entourage* star offer a very similar assessment. "We're all performing in our lives," he told me. "You're creating a role or a character, just like an actor would, and you go through the process of discovery to find out what works and what doesn't. You try things and experiment to find out who your character is and who you want him or her to be, and those experiments inform the final product. When it comes to real life, people think they are what they are and they can't change it, but you're very much making decisions."

Sometimes these performance decisions and moments have an audience of forty thousand, as in the case of a professional athlete—or millions, as in Adrian's case with his television shows and movies—but for you and me they might often be witnessed by only one or maybe two people. In that view there was a certain philosophy applicable to sport that could be trans-ferred to all of your life's moments for both greater success and enhanced enjoyment.

I began to use the *Life as Sport* philosophy and techniques in my own life. As the years passed, I found myself thinking of the *Life as Sport* pillars of enjoyment, present and future orientation, objective optimism, and process focus when I started to feel stress about a particular presentation or relationship challenge.

In this process, a few years back I had a personal awakening that fundamentally changed the way I look at my life.

At age thirty-five I was married, had two children and a successful practice, was a professor in a medical school, and was working as a sport and performance psychologist with some of the most successful athletes and performers of our time. But sometimes I would get bent out of shape whenever the people in my life weren't succeeding in some objective way. Whether they were family members, star athletes, other clients, or employees, I would take on a lot of stress if they were struggling.

I remember talking to one very well-known basketball player whom I had helped in the past and who had been struggling quite a bit. I was discussing the *Life as Sport* philosophy with him when suddenly I realized I wasn't applying it to myself! Despite all of my desire to help him, I couldn't control what the result of our work would be. When I was able to direct my attention to a present focus, practice techniques to move myself beyond what went wrong in the past, enjoy the process by reminding myself about what I enjoyed about working with him, and be positive and optimistic—within reason—I began to feel I was playing in the zone. I felt like an elite athlete playing his or her sport. It was an epiphany for me: *the more that I can treat life in general as a sport, the more effective I will be at it.* If I can treat every presentation, every tough relationship moment, every new endeavor as a sporting event in which I try to focus on what I can control and stick to the *Life as Sport* principles, I will, as a result, succeed more and enjoy the process to a much greater extent.

Above and beyond all the theories and techniques presented, this book will help you treat your work, your relationships, your life just as an elite athlete would treat his sport . . . and by doing so, it will help you win.

Enjoyment Exercise

At the end of every chapter in this book you'll find these "Enjoyment Exercises"—small rituals you can practice not just to get better at the techniques shared in each chapter but also to improve at the critical skill of mindfulness or deepening your connection to the moment. As you'll read, I believe it is extremely important for all of us to seek improvement as well as to enjoy and truly *experience* the journey of improvement. That means taking in and enjoying moments as they pass. These exercises will help you do just that. Here's one to start you off: play the "game within a game." As you're reading this book, try to enjoy competing with yourself about how present you can be while taking in the information. Make it your practice to challenge yourself after each section to see how much information you feel you've retained. You can do this by sharing an idea that you enjoyed from each chapter with a friend. Try to be as specific as possible when you describe your enjoyment to him or her. What was the concept that impacted you, and why?

1

The Life as Sport Philosophy

The *Life as Sport* philosophy has four pillars: enjoyment, present and future orientation, objective optimism, and process focus.

Enjoyment

Champion golfer Jack Nicklaus is famous for saying, "I am a firm believer . . . that people only do their best at things they truly enjoy. It's difficult to excel at something you don't enjoy." With rare exceptions, the athletes I have known who have been able to succeed in the spotlight are those who actually find enjoyment in being there. I remember a long talk I had with Dave Winfield, the Hall of Fame baseball player, who opened my eyes when he discussed his enjoyment of the game. "Jonathan, I was a fierce competitor," he told me. "I remember many moments that stand out as me playing at my best. But the beauty of it is that it's fun. You are outdoors, you have your teammates, you can make a name for yourself. It's a beautiful sport, and part of the beauty is that you never know the outcome. If you learn to embrace this challenge, you can succeed and really enjoy the process at the same time. When I look back, the things I really enjoyed were the same things I enjoyed as a kid—doing something I'd never done before. I was excited about learning and seeing some of the things I learned pay off. I'll always remember the joy of hitting a ball so hard that I knocked the guy's glove off." When Dave spoke to me that day, I could hear his enjoyment of his experience as though he were singing.

World class rugby league player Michael Crocker once told me that his teammates would marvel at the positive energy he could create by dragging all players out into the rain prior to practice to kick balls and slide around in the puddles. "I was excited every day at training because I loved the game, loved training, loved competing, and loved being around my mates. So many young players these days are completely overworked and end up viewing practice as a chore—not a very good mindset to have, and one that definitely impacts on performance and their ability to be at their best. One other thing I did use to promote energy and fun was to sing along to songs when we were doing cardio training in the gym. Sometimes I would completely change the lyrics and turn it into a story about something of relevance to our situation or one of my teammates. I did this because I wanted to enhance my ability to talk out on the field when I was tired or under fatigue. Personally, I feel enjoyment is the key to success in a team environment. You want to be able to laugh and have fun while working as hard as you can. The fulfillment at the end of a tough session or game is when you walk off smiling, knowing that you have done your absolute best and enjoyed it no matter the result."

This does not mean that these people do not get frustrated, occasionally throw their bats, or use mind-blowingly colorful language when they have undesirable results. However, the people who make it and stay in the big leagues of any sport are those who seek out and find satisfaction in some or many aspects of their performance. These men and women are the ones who take great pride in their pre-, during-, and post-performance routines. They are the ones who play the best clubhouse practical jokes, the ones you're still laughing about months after the prank was revealed. These athletes usually build relationships with teammates, staff, and coaches and lead lives full of activity and friendship outside of their profession in organized sports.

In my years interacting with and observing these champions I have witnessed firsthand how powerful their passion for enjoyment is in allowing them to remain consistent in their performance and ride the waves of injury, inconsistent results, and other challenging life circumstances. (I've also gained valuable experience in being the butt of a few practical jokes!) A unifying characteristic of all these players, whether they came from a shack with a dirt floor in Latin America or a twenty-thousand-square-foot mansion in Southern California, was that they were able to look at stressful situations as challenges rather than threats. They were able to find humor in the worst luck and to turn a travel delay into an opportunity to connect with their teammates. As my father always said about any delay on an airplane due to a mechanical issue, "It's infinitely better than the alternative." They were also able to see their outlook not as something innate but instead as a skill to be practiced. The more you practiced this attitude, the more it became you, and then the more it became you, the easier it was to practice it.

After a bad result or a loss, if you were to be in my shoes as a sport psychologist, you'll hear one common reaction by athletes in clubhouses and locker rooms all around the world: "Remember, it's just a game." This reaction helps athletes put things in perspective. When reacting this way to a loss, professional athletes are trying to help themselves avoid getting overwhelmed by the sting of defeat. Sometimes they'll show you a picture of their beautiful girlfriend or insanely cute baby; occasionally they'll talk to you about money in the bank or material possessions. But what they're really trying to do is convince themselves that the loss was not important.

Although this can sometimes help temporarily, it's generally not an effective method of managing their feelings. This is because a negative result in sports or any other arena impacts our self-esteem. We all know that as we are competing for a title, award, or financial success, there are real, life-and-death situations happening out there. But in the context of our lives, the game *does* matter. It *is* important. And although it is "just a game" and our work is "just work," these activities carry with them great personal meaning and have powerful effects on the way we feel about ourselves and, thus, impact the world.

However, these athletes are onto something very powerful. The truly successful athletes look for a way to enjoy their game or sport, win or lose. They find a way to balance the paradox of letting go of the results and returning to the fun of the activity while at the same time mercilessly looking for ways to improve the process that will lead them to their desired outcome.

In the words of the late poker pro Amir Vahedi, "In order to live, you must be willing to die."[1] I have found in working with the most successful athletes that those who can balance their approach to their game by really enjoying the activity while fiercely competing have a higher quality of life, stay in their sport longer, and generally have better results. Paradoxically, if you can give up on the results and just "be," you usually end up with a more successful performance outcome. Dave Winfield also highlighted this concept of play when he told me his version of the well-known story about himself. While he was a Yankee and throwing during a warm-up in a game in Toronto, Dave accidentally hit a seagull with a ball. The gull died, and this caused a stir in the media. Dave told me, "The next series in Detroit, everyone was taunting me, flapping their arms like wings of a bird. They attempted to humiliate and taunt me. But instead of letting it get me down, I used it to motivate me. Every at-bat I hit the ball harder than I ever had. Like a laser beam. Other people might have got frustrated. But I enjoyed seeing how I was going to show those people."

It is this balance that this book will help you achieve. If you can look at your life as a sport and yourself as an elite athlete at the center of this all-important game, you will be able to more easily and effectively achieve the results you desire. The techniques in this book are tools to help you navigate life with this outlook. They are designed to assist you in adopting the most adaptive outlook on life's challenges and developing skills that bring out your best to react to those challenges. You can practice looking at your life as an elite athlete would, determining how to practice these skills in order both to enjoy things more and to achieve greater success.

Many athletes at the end of their careers express regret for having not "enjoyed it more." The "it" that they are talking about usually means the experience of being at the top of their game or just being at the time or place in their life at which they were really having fun, growing, building skills, and developing relationships. In my work with people from all professions, from sports to the performing arts and business, I have found that many people in the late parts of their careers express similar regrets. Part of living life as a sport is attempting to find, every day, ways to increase your level of presence and practice enjoyment. One of the key elements of this is to work on actively being conscious of your level of enjoyment and trying to refocus yourself during your work in improving your skill on this enjoyment.

I've had the privilege of talking with successful veteran athletes as they've looked back on impressive careers sometimes spanning two decades. Most of these athletes are in their last year, dividing their playing time with award ceremonies and parties celebrating their successes. However, some of my most powerful lessons have come from these discussions I've had with veteran athletes in the minor leagues. As you may know, in baseball the minor leagues, or "farm system" as it's sometimes referred to, is the training and development wing of any major league baseball team: players aged sixteen (international draftees, many from Latin America) to their early thirties fighting their way through the upside-down funnel to get to the top of the pyramid and break into the big leagues. When most people think of the minor leagues, they think of eager young rookies recently out of high school or college, full of optimism about their ability to become an All-Star. However, there are a few minor league players, mostly at the highest level (Triple-A), who are former big-leaguers who have come to live out their final years as a baseball player just below the cusp of "the show." They have spent between ten and twenty years playing on a world stage and are now playing in front of forty-seven people in a park that doesn't hold a candle to their big league experience. I've always enjoyed hearing them reflect on their experience, and the primary lesson I've learned is that they wish they stopped to enjoy it more.

Consider this comment that a very successful player in likely the last year of his big league career said to me regarding his biggest regret: "Doc, it just goes by so fast, you know? It's kind of like with your kids, you know? One day they're born a perfect little boy or girl, you close your eyes, and the next second you turn around and they're off to college. Toward the last years there, I was always so focused on getting results, on keeping my numbers up so that I could stay in the big leagues, and I feel like that really hurt me, you know? I became so focused on getting hits that I feel like I lost my love of the game. I always wonder: if I'd just had more fun and just enjoyed being there, if I wouldn't have stayed in a little longer."

This player's reflections match the comments and discussions I've had with many other stars and successful athletes. They all make reference to their desire to have directed more energy toward really enjoying themselves and have commented on their perception that enjoyment leads to better results. As one player said to me recently, "You know how you always tell me, to focus on the self-statement, 'Hit the Mitt' as a way of simplifying my thought process? Well, I feel like that overall about my attitude in being a player. If I'm having fun and focusing on enjoying myself, I tend to stop worrying . . . then I have success and the whole thing kind of fuels itself."

It is easy to lose track of our enjoyment. The stakes in life are high. Whether it's a sport we play or our job or money, our relationship or our kid's well-being on the line, we can easily forget what we love about our activity or our work. We can get carried away in the heat of the moment of a presentation, a work day, a meeting, or a fight with a loved one, only to lose track of our enjoyment of the thing we are working on.

But the best players realize that in order to really be successful and stay that way, you need to practice enjoyment. I think it was said best by Mets right fielder Curtis Granderson, well known for his friendly, playful, but professional nature: "The game's still got to be the same way as when you played it when you were a little kid. Because if it's fun, then you're going to want to work, and once you work, then you start to get the results, and once you get the results, that's more fun again, and that cycle continues all over again."[2]

One technique I share with athletes that has been successful in helping them to refocus on enjoying is the "ME" concept. The M stands for *Motivation* and the E stands for *Enjoyment*. Before each important activity, meeting, or event, athletes I work with will go through a routine in which they remind themselves to "put the ME into it." That is, they clarify their motivation and keep it close to their consciousness and then practice enjoyment.

By the time they are playing or performing, this process is so ingrained that they don't actively think about it. They have a mental shorthand to double-check that they have paid attention that day to their motivation and enjoyment. For example, they can flash their motivation through their mind or look at their motivation reminder (we will cover these techniques in detail in Chapter 3, Motivation). Enjoyment can also be practiced (see the How-To section at the end of this chapter). Throughout this book we will explore ways that you can use the ME technique to practice the art of enjoyment as a way of improving your process. Each chapter will give you a specific exercise to help you seize each moment in your life, being mindful to really live it fully, the same way an elite athlete would in a championship game. I agree with most of the successful athletes that I have talked to, that working to enjoy your life is a surefire way to achieve the best results and the highest level of satisfaction that *you* are capable of.

Objective Optimism

I tend to meet two kinds of people. The first believe in the power of positive thinking. They have Facebook and Twitter pages full of inspirational quotes, look at things as a "glass half full," and can find the upside to nearly any situation. The others are those who think that optimism and positivity are dangerous. They believe that "too positive" an outlook is dangerous in that optimists might overlook important and real negative information about themselves and their environment that is necessary to make essential changes in becoming their optimal selves. These people also seem to have a special type of gene that makes them want to throw up whenever they see a motivational quote.

There is a third way of looking at things, one that I call "objective optimism." Rather than decide whether you'll see the glass as half empty or half full, assume it's half full and work backward from there. In other words, if you're in the position to look at the situation with unclear information about yourself, your performance, or other important situations, try to have an "innocent until proven guilty" attitude rather than a "guilty until proven innocent" attitude. Optimism and positivity are hugely important and influential forces on our expectations and views of ourselves that lead to optimal performance. However, the optimism that I see in successful athletes almost always comes out of an organic objective analysis of their situation. These athletes work to look for proof of how they are excellent, not how they "suck." In the end it is your outlook that determines your experience and, thus, your performance. As Shakespeare wrote, "There is nothing either good or bad but thinking makes it so."

Over the years I've been shocked by how many high-level athletes struggle with their outlook. Many who were facing with slumps or suboptimal performances came to me, seeking out my counsel, but with little to no awareness of just how much negative information they're feeding themselves. Despite their talent and impressive success, world-class athletes are no different from any of us. They tend to be very affected by negative results and lack inherent philosophies to battle back against this self-driven negative feedback.

Now, put this athlete with a pessimistic or negative philosophy on a team with a critical teammate or coach or a stadium with forty thousand hostile fans, and you've got a recipe for disaster. What I teach athletes is a philosophy that I aim to teach you in this book: to begin to seek out evidence that you're okay, that the world is okay, and that the results will be okay. Which house will you live a more successful life in—the house overlooking an expansive ocean view or the shack in the middle of junkyard? Clearly the way in which you look at yourself will determine how well you can compete and your overall enjoyment of your experience. With the elite performers I work with, I call this crucial viewpoint your "In-Look," as you are really examining and messaging yourself internally rather than really looking out at the world.

One crucial caveat: this is not just positive thinking! There is a major distinction between positive thinking (i.e., "I'm going to kick ass in this presentation!") vs. objective optimism ("I'm going to do well in this presentation because I have done well in the previous three presentations, I am prepared, and I have received favorable feedback on my skills."). Whenever possible, it is essential to be positive and find a way to focus on objective evidence for this positivity. Your evidence must be based on fact or else your brain will reject it.

As my good friend and fellow sport psychology expert Dr. Derick Anderson says, "You can't teach a dog to sit by saying, 'Don't stand!'" Invariably, human beings focus on what's going wrong. However, we shouldn't blame ourselves for this tendency, as it is evolutionarily wired. Studies have shown that the amygdala—a tiny almond-shaped lobe in your brain responsible for memory, emotion, and decision making—reacts more strongly to negative news than positive news, leaping to exaggerate the faintest possibility of negativity, fear, and failure, like a neurological alarm bell that rings out at the slightest provocation.[3] Biologically, perhaps out of an age-old instinct for self-preservation, we are primed to linger on the negative. Let's look at this in more detail.

Our nervous system has been evolving for hundreds of millions of years. In doing so, it has been designed to help us survive. Our nervous system is on constant lookout for danger. Our ancestors needed to know if a hungry lion was around the corner—and fast! We were always looking to hunt ourselves, but we could survive two or three days without a rabbit. However, it takes only one lion to end all your days of hunting. In that way fear is a very powerful agent in our behaviors. We are wired to be fearful and alert.[4] This is sometimes called a negative bias—it's why phobias of survival-related dangers like snakes or heights are so readily learned and why they persist across a wide cultural, historical, and geographical swath of the human race.[5] All things being equal, your brain looks for what's wrong, not what's right.

Think about it this way: when you're walking down a dark alley in a foreign city, how much time do you spend concerning yourself with being mugged by an elderly person with a cane? Or do you spend your time looking for the muscular person with a ski mask charging at you with a knife? We are built to look for the thing that's out of place in our environment and in our life. We tend to notice the strikeout but not the double, the grade of C but not the A.

You might ask, "Why is that a problem? Don't I need to keep myself on my toes by pointing out what I'm not doing well? Doesn't that motivate me to do better?"

Well, as it turns out, no, not really. The reality is that when it comes to peak performance—that is, performing at our best—we're much better off figuring out what's going well and continuing to foster those positive changes rather than constantly replaying negative results and situations. This much is borne out by a recent study of elite table tennis players: concentrating on the present, not the past, was crucial to their ability to reach the psychological state for peak performance.[6]

As far as peak performance goes in sports, business, performing arts, and other areas of life, the most effective sport psychology focuses on understanding what is working and building on that. This is the most robust way to build up your confidence. When you learn the techniques of self-talk (Chapter 6) and managing anxiety (Chapter 4), you will have tools to overcome your natural fear and tendency to notice the negative more than the positive. This ability to be positive when appropriate will help you develop the optimal attitude to compete and succeed in all aspects of your life.

Present and Future Orientation

The tradition in psychology has often been focused on what went wrong in the past. We are often trying to find out why something bad happened to us: What was wrong with our upbringing or lack of preparation that might explain why we haven't met our goals or are in an unfavorable position in life?

In our worst moments we may even tell ourselves that our past decisions and circumstances have led us to "being a person who can't _____." I remember a conversation I was having with a basketball player, Ronny, who was extremely anxious in social situations. Whenever he had to do an interview he would feel so nervous that he would sometimes have to make an emergency trip to the bathroom before it began! I remember talking to him about some anxiety he had in dating or being with women: "Doc, I don't know. I've always been like this . . . since I was in junior high. Whenever I'm around people, especially women, and I have to, you know, talk, I feel like my face is going to get so hot that it's gonna explode." (Incidentally, what this player was discussing was feeling symptoms of physiological arousal—the body's feelings of anxiety. We will cover how to manage these sensations in Chapter 4, on managing anxiety, as they come up to some degree for most of us in times of pressure during performance.)

The player went on to tell me this about his past orientation: "I've tried to change. Hell, I've even taken meds to make it go away. But it's just who I am, who I grew up to be, who I have always been—an anxious person."

I responded by telling him that I don't believe in the existence of "anxious people."

He was shocked at my reply. Stunned, he looked at me incredulously. I continued to explain: "Ronny, there is no such thing as an anxious person. Only people who experience anxiety."

When you begin to think of the way you are as stable or permanent, or of your past as the determining factor in your life, you are destined to a life where change is difficult, if not impossible, where your goals are always eclipsed by your fixed, global, and past-based self-concept. What you can do is what Ronny eventually did: work to break free of the past and to change your outlook to be more present and future focused. The *Life as Sport* philosophy helps you realize that the one part of your life that you have no control over is your past. Many professional athletes make a mistake—give up a run, strike out, miss a foul shot—and become so bothered by what happened in the immediate past that their present and future performance is not anything like what they are capable of. We have all seen it in sports: a world-class athlete falls apart after making one crucial blunder.

Sam Kass played baseball at a high level in college, but his athletic accomplishments were overshadowed by his activities in the culinary arts and as a leader in nutrition in government. Sam served under President Barack Obama as a senior policy adviser for nutrition policy and as executive director for First Lady Michelle Obama's *Let's Move!* campaign. He and I have had some lively discussions about what he learned from baseball and how some of the *Life as Sport*–type thinking played a part in his success. "I think focusing on the present is one of the key lessons that baseball taught me that helped me in being a chef," he told me. "I failed so often in baseball. It's a game of failure. If you do not learn how to learn from the past and overcome it to focus on the task at hand, you're not going to stand a chance. If you fail seven out of ten times in your baseball career, you're going to be a Hall-of-Famer. That sport experience really taught me to focus on the task at hand in my culinary work and not on the past or future. When I first started cooking for the Obamas I stayed focused on excelling in each moment, and those moments led to a life-changing opportunity. I had been interested in food and politics, but if I hadn't really put in the work and practiced a present orientation, I might have been the White House cook but never would have been able to help shape a massive national health campaign."

You are no different. In your sporting life, business life, social and romantic lives, you can frequently become fixated on a mistake or loss that, if you are unable to move beyond it, can become very costly with regard to your present or future performance.

Throughout the book you will meet people like Ronny and Sam, and I will show you the ways in which I worked with them to have a present and future orientation. Most research and my experience suggest that having a mindful engagement with the present moment has a host of performance and health benefits.[7] The reason I include future orientation in this principle of the philosophy is that some of the aspects of the techniques that we will master together, such as goal setting, involve the future. That said, most of the focus of the techniques and philosophies herein pertain to focusing on what you can do in the present moment to move yourself closer to your goals, whatever they might be. Whether you are working on becoming less anxious in your sport, improving your ability to navigate a social situation, or trying to master a certain job role, we will work together to bring your energy toward improving on the things you have control over right here and now. As the Dalai Lama wisely said, "There are only two days in the year that nothing can be done. One is called Yesterday and the other is called Tomorrow. Today is the right day to Love, Believe, Do and mostly Live."

Yuri Foreman is an internationally known boxer and former WBA super welterweight champion. He certainly knows the power of being in the present moment:

Being in the moment is the most important thing in boxing. All your attention has to be focused on your opponent. I never concentrate on throwing more punches or punching harder. I divert my attention away from the end result and try to immerse myself in the moment. The closest thing I can compare it to is meditation. When you sit there quietly and focus on your breath, you feel everything. I think that's why meditation has helped me. Once, in a crucial fight, I got a bad cut over my eye. I couldn't see, and the opponent I was facing was very strong. I lost my focus. My cut man—the guy patching me up—was concerned and working furiously to fix my wound the best he could. I began to panic a little. My trainer, a very calm, spiritual guy, wasn't fazed. He said, "You are fine, son. This is nothing. You are going to jab in the face, and he won't be able to touch you."

That really got me back into the moment. The fight was more difficult because I made it difficult. I made the opponent larger and more powerful than he really was. When you make the images of your opponent or obstacles in your head, make sure you cut them to size. Once I did that in that fight, I was able to overcome the cut, and thus the opponent. Fight like that in your life, and you will, too.

You will learn to build routines (Chapter 7) that refocus you on the present moment instead of belaboring a past negative result. You will work on enhancing your self-talk (Chapter 6) in order to provide you with strategies for speaking to yourself and reorienting away from unhelpful thinking and onto a more effective thought process. You will learn ways of shifting focus by asking yourself, "How will worrying about what just happened help me?" Sooner than you think, the person you were will fade away, and the parts of your personality that want to look forward, toward the person you want to be, will emerge. The more you can fully engage in the moment and allow yourself to be fully present in the experience, the more likely that your best "stuff" will come to the surface. A winning mind-set is having the willingness to accept all of your feelings and then refocus on what you can do right now. The more you fight to change things that are out of your control, the deeper into quicksand you sink. Many times the self-talk I use with players is simply to say the words "This pitch" or "this moment" as a way to center themselves. I also frequently ask the panicked trader and the frustrated parent, "What can we do right now?" One central way to stay effective in the present moment is to concentrate on the process instead of the outcome.

Process Focus

"Doc, I just need you to help me get my batting average up. Can't you do that?!"

Most athletes approach me at a point in their career when, despite their strong history of hitting home runs or stellar fielding or striking out batters, they find themselves in a serious slump. Their batting average has plummeted, or they are walking everyone, or they are becoming known for their errors in the field. With my help, these athletes learn that they need to control the controllables. What can they actively control in a situation?

Most people—including athletes and nonathletes alike—tend to focus on the results. For athletes it might be to make more touchdowns or swim faster laps. To strike out more batters or to shoot three-pointers. To jump higher or to check harder. For the rest of us maybe it is to make more money, find a romantic partner, lose weight, or have more measurable success in business or sports. The first simple yet revolutionary step we all need to take is to accept the fact that we have no direct control over those results. After all, we can't just will ourselves to make more money or find a new romantic partner or start striking people out. There are simply far too many variables outside of our control that will affect our chances of achieving those goals.

The results you seek are best obtained by taking your focus off the results and developing a focus on your process. By intertwining substantial theories with practical techniques, the book will help you develop the process of a champion.

What is most successful for any individual is to focus on what actions are most likely to lead to the results we want. If our goal is to raise our batting average, then we need to take our focus off the average itself and instead direct our experimentation around this process: to ascertain what routines, strategies, and thought processes will most likely lead to our desired outcome or results. We look to create a mind-set that produces quality at-bats.

Another thing we can control is our cognitive and behavioral reaction to any stressful or unwanted result. In my work with baseball players, if a player strikes out, I help them learn to use positive self-talk (which we will cover in Chapter 6) in order to think in a helpful way about their performance. Rather than just lamenting that they didn't get that hit, I ask them to observe what they did to have a quality at-bat. Did they see the ball well when it was coming out of the pitcher's release point? Did they make good contact despite fouling off the pitch? Were they criticizing themselves for hitting it directly to an outfielder when the outfielder's position was clearly out of their control? In fact, one of the central themes of this book, control the controllables, is precisely about how to avoid this problem: how to notice when you are focusing too much on results that may be partly or even entirely outside of your control and how to divert your energy to strategizing how to improve your approach or your reactions. Note that I said you can control how you react in your cognitions (thoughts) and your behaviors (reactions); you cannot control your emotions directly. They are a result just like a batting average, report card, or a profit-and-loss summary.

Similarly, to apply this to life outside of sports, most of us—if not all of us—are interested in making more money. I see it in my practice, where clients complain about their financial situation or fantasize incessantly about financial independence. But although most of us may want more money, the acts of constantly monitoring bank accounts, complaining about not having enough, or wishing we had more can't ever create wealth. Because obsessing over an outcome doesn't make that outcome happen.

Instead, I encourage you to take your mind off of the results and move it toward your actions—for example, having realistic and measurable goals (to be discussed in Chapter 2), using positive imagery (to be discussed in Chapter 5), and employing positive self-talk (to be discussed in Chapter 6) are far more effective strategies in our approach that should lead to the desired results, whether it be making more money or getting more hits.

Bobby Cannavale has built an impressive career in television and movies, winning his share of critical acclaim, including two Primetime Emmy Awards for his work on *Boardwalk Empire* and *Will and Grace*. He stars in the upcoming HBO series *Vinyl*. Bobby tells me that acting and auditioning are like a sport. "I can only work on the things I control in the process, being enthusiastic and visualizing how I want to perform and what I want to get out of the moment," he said. "The more enthusiasm I show and the more present I am in that moment, the more people will be attracted to what I am doing as an actor."

Although the concept of having a process focus is probably becoming more clear, how to do it may still be elusive. I have found that when athletes are in the moment, concrete and easy sound bites help them remember and put into practice the important concepts and strategies I have taught them. If you're fielding a ball—or trading on the stock market or are out on a date—it's going to be hard to think back to this initial chapter and remember the concept of focusing on the process instead of the results.

So I have created an acronym that will keep your attention on our system of focusing on actions and reactions (the process) rather than the outcome (result). I encourage the athletes and other high performers I work with to "Stay on the DOT," where DOT stands for DOING, OUTCOME, THINKING. The figure represents each component of the DOT concept. Let's examine each of the letters one at a time.

The D, for *Doing*, corresponds to some of the strategies you will learn in this book in order to increase your peak performance or the time you spend staying in "the zone," a place in which your high ability meets a high challenge successfully. In most performance settings in life and sports, having a plan, practicing it, and putting it into place is the quickest path toward getting the results you want. The strategies in this book will not only allow you to sharpen your ability to make that plan but will also help you make sure your actions are as effective as possible. In the illustration of the DOT model you can see that the athlete lifting weights represents an action toward a result. Similarly there are strategies you will learn in the chapters to come that will help you to develop actions that will impact the outcomes in your life. These strategies are depicted above the barbells (visualization, breathing, training, and routines). Second, let's jump ahead to the T in DOT. *Thinking* is critical: how we think about or react to both positive and negative results and upcoming challenges, in both sport and life performance, can contribute to our ability to perform at our best. This part of the DOT is represented here by the figure who is approaching the finish line. If at the end of a race, or during an important event or meeting, you interpret your behavior, or feelings in your body in an incorrect or negative way, you inhibit your ability to perform at your best. This is just as true whether you're on a pitching mound, in front of a podium, or participating in a military or law enforcement operation. Also crucial is that many performers are inhibited by thinking at the wrong time. Many situations involving high-performance

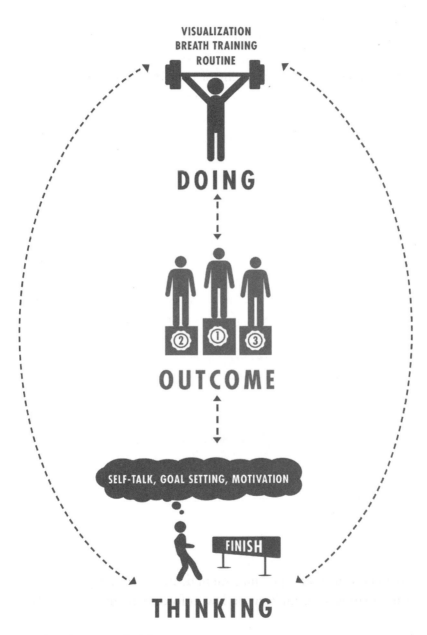

VISUALIZATION
BREATH TRAINING
ROUTINE

DOING

OUTCOME

SELF-TALK, GOAL SETTING, MOTIVATION

FINISH

THINKING

demands are not compatible with thinking. They are situations in which you should be so practiced that thoughts become irrelevant and you rely completely on your practiced actions or routine. By introducing you to Self-Talk, Goal Setting, and Motivational Enhancement, this book will help you assess which situations demand an enhanced cognitive strategy and how to quiet your mind and build your power in spite of stress, fear, or anxiety.

Finally, the O stands for *Outcome*. It is depicted here in the result of coming in first, second, or third place in a competition. I've actually placed it last in our discussion for a reason. When people meet with me in my practice I often ask them one important question: "If I turned out to be the most helpful doctor for you, how would your life change as a result of our work together?" One of the main reasons I ask this question is so we begin the conversation in a way that focuses on what they want to do and not what is wrong with their life. If we have a positive focal point, it makes goal setting more powerful and attainable.

Most answers in some way encompass results that have to do with happiness and life satisfaction. Yet people are often shocked when I proceed to tell them that we have no control over whether they obtain these results. Quickly and before they run out of the door, I explain what I mean. As I mentioned before, we have no direct control over any outcome or result in our life, be it happiness, satisfaction, health, wealth, or striking out the side. What we do control is our mental preparation in our actions and our reactions—and that will dictate the quality of and degree to which we reach our personal goals. This book will be your gym and training camp, helping you train your brain to focus on what you have control over: your actions and your reactions—what you do and what you think.

In order to get them into a game mentally and to help them let go of the outcome, I encourage my clients to adopt the mentality of an ancient warrior. We succeed when we can act freely, when we do not allow fear to rule our actions, judgment, or our state of mind. The ancient Japanese warriors, the Samurai, went into battle with a complete acceptance of the possibility of dying. Their demise was of no concern; their focus was singular: to give their all in battle, to live in that moment. Neither victory nor defeat had any meaning, only the performance of one's duty to the best of one's ability. Similarly, it's our goal to work with players to allow them to focus on the battle, not the results. Yes, like a Samurai warrior, if we head into a pursuit accepting that failure is as much a possibility as success, we allow ourselves to focus instead on our performance. In all sports and in life in general, we win when we attend to our contributions, when we are well armed not just physically but also mentally, when we are prepared to give all and eschew obsessing over how everything will turn out. In other words, when we accept and overcome all of our internal mental obstacles, our real-life barriers and competitors are no match for us. It should be noted that there are arrows in this illustration going from outcome to doing and thinking, and from thinking to doing, and doing to thinking. This is because what we do and what we think affect each other. Certainly outcomes can affect our thoughts, but also, as we will learn later, what we do can affect our thoughts, and what we think can affect what we do. Focusing on developing a well-honed process that helps you to think and act in the most adaptive way possible will allow you enjoy yourself and achieve the best outcomes possible.

In this book we will cover the different techniques people use to achieve this process-focused mentality. As mentioned, one strategy is to use self-talk, which will be covered in more detail in Chapter 6. By thinking about things in terms of positive self-statements, like "I am doing well overall" and "I've gotten as far as I have because . . . ," we help ourselves let go of the outcome, allowing us to fully immerse in the game.

It is often challenging to change your focus from having this process focus in practice to being fully present with the pressures of game time. As we will learn in Chapter 7, it is helpful to build a practice routine. We might tell ourselves to stop worrying, but often our mind doesn't respond to our mental commands. By establishing a routine between practice and game time, your body becomes programmed to know it's time to do and not think. For example, a tennis player may bounce a ball a few times before she serves. A batter might tighten his batting glove several times before he stands at the plate. These actions regulate us and help our mind let go of thoughts, fears, and worries. It will help you ask yourself in every situation: "Am I 'on the DOT?' How much am I focusing on what I can control in this situation?" The more you make this analysis part of your routine, the more you will succeed.

Bryan Cranston, star of the hit television show *Breaking Bad*, really knows how to stay on the DOT. He explained how having a process focus is important in finding success as a performer. "The best advice for fellow actors is this: know what your job is. I was going into auditioning, trying to get a job, and that wasn't what I was supposed to be doing. An actor is supposed to create a compelling interest in the character that serves the text, presented in the environment where your audition happens, and then you walk away. And that's it. Everything else is out of your control, so don't even think of it. Don't focus on that. You're not going there to get a job. You're there to present what you do. You act. And there it is. Walk away. There is power in that. There is confidence in that . . . then the decision of who might get a job is so out of your control that when you analyze it, it makes no sense to hold onto that. That to me was a breakthrough. And once I adapted that philosophy, I never looked back. And I've never been busier in my life than once I grabbed onto that."

Your Road Map

To establish these four pillars of *Life as Sport* in your own life we're going to take a systematic, step-by-step approach. In the next chapter you'll learn how to set goals in a way that inspires and promotes performance instead of the damaging way most people do it. Chapter 3 is dedicated to understanding and taking advantage of your built-in, internal sense of motivation. By carefully curating and calibrating your goals and the steps you take toward those goals, you'll never need to worry about low motivation again.

Anxiety derails athletes in the biggest moments of their career—and is just as damaging in smaller-stakes, day-to-day situations we all face. Chapter 4 will show you how to identify anxiety and both reduce it as well as use the residuals of it for heightened performance.

Visualization is another catch word you've probably heard athletes use when talking about their preparation—both before a season and before an important sequence within a game. It's a skill that has use far beyond the field or court. In Chapter 5 I'll show you how to develop your own visualization skills and feel success before it happens. You don't have to buy into Eastern philosophy to benefit from a "mantra." In Chapter 6 you'll learn how to understand and control your self-talk—the internal monologue you have with yourself. By learning how to create your own kind of self-statement, or mantra, you can take control of your thought patterns and direct your moods to a more positive place. You've probably heard athletes talk

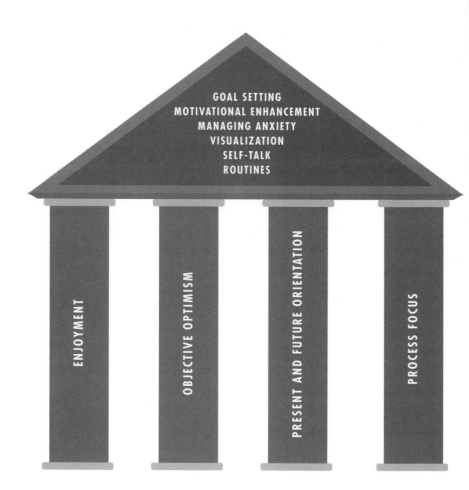

GOAL SETTING
MOTIVATIONAL ENHANCEMENT
MANAGING ANXIETY
VISUALIZATION
SELF-TALK
ROUTINES

ENJOYMENT

OBJECTIVE OPTIMISM

PRESENT AND FUTURE ORIENTATION

PROCESS FOCUS

LIFE AS SPORT PHILOSOPHY SUPPORTS THE TECHNIQUES

about following a routine to calm the mind; in Chapter 7 you'll learn how to establish a useful routine for yourself and how to access it.

In the last segment we'll bring it all together. The Conclusion is dedicated to setting you on the course to a more aware, mindful experience of living in the moment, like a big league pitcher does as he's getting ready to release the payoff pitch in the ninth inning of a playoff game.

In summary, the *Life as Sport* philosophy consists of the ideas or general attitudes that elite athletes and performers use to view life as a challenge, not as a threat. It is a mind-set that allows them to pull the best from themselves. By adhering to this philosophy, you build a sturdy structure with which to practice the strategies in this book. The philosophy supports the techniques that you will learn in each chapter. To reinforce this concept, you can see the four pillars of the Life as Sport philosophy illustrated on page 26. Note the philosophical pillars support the roof that contain the sport psychology techniques you will learn in the following six chapters.

Even the best information is useful only if you can apply it to your own life. My goal is not only to explain the *Life as Sport* philosophy and accompanying skills but also to give you simple, practical ways to build and apply those skills. At the end of each chapter (and this introduction) you'll find a How-To section with specific, actionable exercises and drills you can follow to incorporate the chapter's concepts. These are the same techniques and exercises I use in every session with a professional athlete. They clarify the message and keep you accountable for the next steps. These exercises will help you truly engage with the concepts in the *Life as Sport* philosophy, whether you are designing a new workflow for your business, working to inspire a team or individual, or even falling in love. This, to me, is what it means to truly live life as a sport: to approach it with the same immediacy, wonder, and engagement that athletes feel at their peak during a game. The practice will help you pursue your own goals with an enriched intensity—not only because it gives you new potential but also because it helps you unlock what was always there to begin with.

A hush falls over the crowd, a whistle blows, a flurry of movement—*game on*.

Enjoyment Exercise

Sit for five minutes with your eyes closed and imagine what it will feel like to achieve your life goals. Use your imagination to really set the stage in your mind for your eventual success. Imagine your life unfold in the way you would like it to with regard to your goal. See the important people in your life react to your success. Use all your senses to vividly imagine the thoughts, feelings, and sensations you will experience with the enjoyment of those moments. Do not hold back. Imagine yourself more successful than you have ever been. Deepen your enjoyment for that success in your mind. Try to feel the excitement that will come as you visualize your realization of your potential.

2

Setting Goals:
Building a Mastery Map

Baseball players are laid bare in a way that few of us will ever experience.

Imagine walking into your place of work on a hot summer day, getting ready to do something you've been training to do your entire life. Tens of thousands of people are in the crowd, watching you as you work. A giant scoreboard in your office flashes your productivity statistics for the year and the day— showing the relative success (or lack of it) you've had. Those same statistics get broadcast across the bottom of the television screens, superimposed over your image around the world.

And all of this happens even before you go about the business of trying to start your day.

Baseball, with all of its obscure statistics and measurements of everything the human body can do on the field, provides such a clear barometer for "success." Getting a hit three times out of ten means you're batting .300 (getting a hit 30 percent of the time)—a notable achievement. But when you get a hit two times out of those same ten at-bats on average, your batting average drops to .200—and it might be time to start worrying about somebody taking your job.

And when you look up at the Jumbotron and see a batting average of .200 next to your name blown up in thousand-point type, you can feel your uniform getting hotter with each swing. That's the time when many players start to get lost in the quicksand of a slump. They're concentrating so hard on trying to break the slump that they're getting in their own way.

Over the years I've talked to many ballplayers in the midst of that struggle, and the conversations often have a similar tone.

"I don't know, Doc. It feels like I'm never gonna get another hit."

"I'm just so focused on hitting the ball. It's all I can think about."

"I know I'm fielding well, but I can't stay at this level if I don't bring my average up."

"I keep changing my swing and making adjustments, but nothing seems to work."

"I've gotta get a hit in this game."

It's natural to think of high-achieving athletes as super-driven and mostly immune to the crises of confidence that can affect "regular" people. You want to think of your athletic heroes as people with a meticulously planned set of goals, solid motivation to achieve them, and extra-stout resolve to push through any obstacles.

But that isn't always the case.

Like anybody, professional athletes and high achievers in all walks of life make the mistake of not building productive goals or become obsessed with goals that actively hurt their performance.

One of the most common responses I get when I ask slumping players what their goals are is some variation of "I just want

to start hitting better" or "I just want to start throwing better."
But wanting something isn't the same as making a plan for it to
actually happen. "I just want to _____ better" isn't a functional or efficient goal.

Setting goals based on outcomes like "pitching better" or
"striking more people out" or "getting better at sales calls" or
"making clients more satisfied" or "being a better parent/partner"
is far less effective than building a set of goals based on processes—
goals that deepen our appreciation for the steps that need to be
taken on the way to achieving the goal, both in practice and in
competition.

That might sound like a good, common-sense approach, but
there's more behind it than just conventional wisdom. A variety
of comprehensive, long-range studies have established that stra-
tegic goal setting has a strong positive impact on results in
sports, business, and other settings. In sports specifically, athletes have been using the techniques we're about to talk about
for decades to reduce stress and improve performance.[1]

As far as the human brain is concerned, consistently hitting
a 95-mile-per-hour fastball or increasing revenue by 10 percent in the next fiscal year aren't as different as you might
think. They're both difficult tasks that require a clear objective
goal that informs skill development, practice, concentration,
and efficient decision making. In other words, as far as the
goal is concerned, the brain views those sports and business
tasks in the same way. This means we can use the same goal-
setting tools for the job.

One of the boilerplate tools I use with all of my performance
clients—whether they're athletes, stock traders, musicians or
authors—is the **DOT** exercise introduced in the previous chapter, which encourages you to identify the three components of
your performance experience and focus on two of three things:

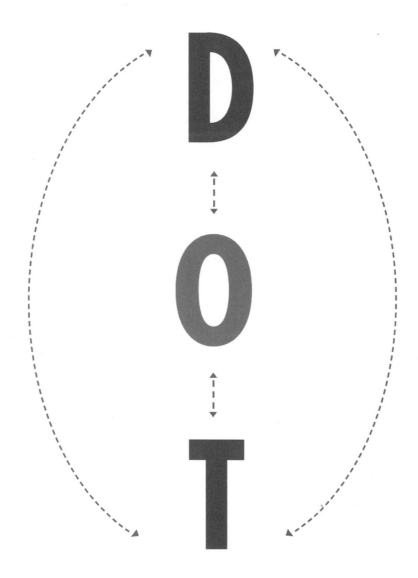

A batting average, test grade, bonus figure, how many dates you line up on an online site, or closing a deal are all outcomes. They're results, outcomes that are influenced by factors that may not be within your direct control. Much of the work of this chapter will require you to figure out how you can redirect your efforts, to focus on the D and the T in your goal setting and, thus, in your performance. What can you do differently and how can you think about the wide variety of potential outcomes in order to perform at your best?

In essence this chapter is about setting the right goals—ones that will help you achieve whatever it is that you want, on whichever field it is you're playing on. We're going to talk about the anatomy of well-built, functional, and efficient goals, and I'll show you how to create—and, when necessary—modify them for yourself.

Goals 101

The boilerplate definition of a goal—a physical or mental performance target—is simple enough. But what goes into effective goal identifying and goal setting is more complex. How do you build a goal that is challenging enough to both inspire you to dedicate your effort and focus that effort in the right direction, but not so challenging or broad that it can make you give up or ignore it?

When I worked with mostly minor league players I heard plenty of nineteen- or twenty-year-olds talk about their goals for the upcoming season. They'd say something like they wanted to come out and hit so many home runs that the big club would have to notice and move them up or that they were going to strike out twelve guys in their next start.

But in the baseball world there are two halves to every equation. A batter can stand in the box feeling confident and strong, and he can read the pitcher like a book and make perfect contact on the exact pitch he was expecting to see. That ball can go flying out of the stadium for a home run, or it could turn out to be a laser beam that unluckily finds its way straight into the glove of the centerfielder for a disappointing out.

The same holds true for the pitcher. He can get the sign from the catcher—a two-seam fastball just off the low outside corner—and execute his pitch exactly the way he planned. He can have the batter completely fooled. Either it could produce a swing and a miss, or the fooled hitter could make a weak check swing and hit a dribbler that the second baseman can't quite reach.

Those two examples reveal the serious limitations of outcome-based goals. They don't take into consideration factors that are outside of your control, and they run a large risk of causing you to feel discouraged because they don't offer a sophisticated way to measure subtle inputs.

For example, how would that pitcher judge his performance if his goal is to strike out twelve guys, and instead he throws eight scoreless innings, induces a bunch of ground balls, but strikes out only six? Or what if he blows those twelve guys away, but he gives up three home runs in the second inning and doesn't execute his pitches the way he wants in a bunch of other tight situations?

How about the person who is a part of a sales team who has a record year, qualifying everybody in the group for a large bonus? What if that one person in the group didn't have a great plan for building relationships and struggled to make new contacts. Judging on outcome—the bonus check in his or her account—it was a great year. But without some kind of process change, the struggling salesperson won't be able to sustain the improvement that needs to happen the next year or over the long term.

Take a step back and think about the goals you want to achieve, whether in your work or relationships. Maybe you're trying to get the next promotion at work or you want to buy a new home. Ask yourself the following questions to get an initial assessment of the quality of your goal:

Is it a process goal (your target is an action/reaction) vs. outcome goal (result)?

How much is your goal affected by things you don't control?

How are you monitoring your goal (i.e., measuring your success)?

How clear are the plans you have to achieve your goal?

We've talked about why process goals are more effective than outcome goals, but what do process goals really look like?

Let's start with the example of a baseball hitter. The primary things a hitter can control are his preparation and his mind-set. He can do all the things baseball hitters have at their disposal to know what an opposing pitcher's tendencies are—and what his own strengths and weaknesses are. Instead of making an outcome goal such as, "I'm going to get a hit today," a hitter can say, "I will make sure I know what this pitcher throws and how

I think he's going to try to get me out. I will make sure I'm relaxed in the box and I am attacking one pitch at a time."

Beyond that preparation the hitter can be doing all of the other things we will be discussing in other chapters to be prepared in the big picture—relaxation techniques to manage anxiety (Chapter 4), positive self-talk (Chapter 6), and visualization (Chapter 5). The hitter can then tie in a series of goals to his own preparation and be able to say to himself—with conviction—that he did everything he could do to be ready to hit. At that point the results take care of themselves. The pitcher might throw a particularly nasty backdoor slider that moves away from his relaxed, measured swing and gets him out, or the batter might take advantage of a pitcher's good pitch that just hung up there a little too long and got just enough of the ball to rip a double into the right field gap. Over time judging himself on how well he follows his process is what will not only improve the quality of each at-bat and maximize the chances for positive results but also free him from the tension that comes from getting caught up in the results themselves.

Turn on any sporting event on television and you can see this play out on both the positive and negative ends of the spectrum. A player in the midst of a bad slump will often come up and anxiously lunge at pitches, trying desperately to "make something happen." When it fails—and it usually does—you'll see him slam the helmet down and tear off the batting glove as he gets ready to go back into the field, disgust written all over his face like the critical headlines of their local newspaper. It might look like the player is just blowing off some steam, but what it really does is cause a cycle of anger and frustration that makes it harder to play in the ideal, relaxed state the next time up.

I work with players to create a different set of process-oriented goals that aren't related to getting hits or getting hitters out. For example, we'll establish a set way for a hitter to react if he crushes a ball but it gets snared by a fielder making a great play. Instead of reacting angrily and saying "I got robbed!" the player responds calmly and realistically. "I got my pitch and I hit it hard. I did my job." Instead of being consumed by the anxiety-producing goal of trying to get a hit every time up, the player is focusing on the goal of reacting to what happens in an even, observational way. This player will get into the batter's box refreshed and ready to hit in his next turn up, avoiding weighing himself down with a bunch of critical thoughts for his next opportunity. All at-bats, all presentations, all relationships are independent chances for success unless you are bringing negative stories about what happened to you previously into the present moment. The objective of a well-constructed goal in baseball—being relaxed rather than hitting a home run—is that it enables you to really have a present and future focus and gives you the best chance to succeed in the most important moment: *this one*.

The process works the same way outside sports. One of my clients came to me after spending many years working on the trading desk for a large Wall Street firm. He recently had started trading on his own, and when we first met he talked with simultaneous frustration and excitement about his main goal—making $30,000 per month. The goal was causing him a tremendous amount of stress because it was far more than he had yet produced and he was finding that he often didn't have control over the results. On a rough day in the market he might show a small loss—but the fact that it was only a small loss compared to some of the beatings his colleagues took was actually a success.

In our first meeting I asked him what his ideal state of mind would be when he was making great trades and progressing toward that $30,000 number. What would be the ideal way to "be"? He thought about it for a second and then said that when he was trading in "the zone" and trading well, he felt calm and masterful. He described it as "glazing"—like the character Neo in the *Matrix* movies. It felt like he was floating in the middle of all his data and was making calm, quick, nonjudgmental decisions.

I helped him set some goals unrelated to that $30,000 number that were designed to measure how well he put himself in position to get to that "glazing" state. We created an enjoyment target and a calmness target—subjective ratings of his calmness while he was trading. Using skills we're going to talk about later in the book—adaptive thinking (Chapter 6, Self-Talk) and breathing (Chapter 4, Managing Anxiety)— this ambitious trader practiced developing calmness at his desk. He would take a moment several times each day to actually pause and grade himself on how he was meeting his enjoyment and calmness targets.

Just taking the step to monitor those two metrics was by itself enough to change his behavior. He had some other work to do, but the big first step was the monitoring part because it prevented him from being able to avoid the issue—and avoidance is the mortal enemy of success. If you put yourself in a situation where you can avoid a problem and ignore the consequences to it, you're creating a negative circuit that will make it very hard to accomplish your goals. The more you make mistakes and fail, the less you want to think about those mistakes. That causes you to avoid the things that will help you make better decisions, in turn producing more negative avoidance feelings. As we will discuss shortly, making clear and functional goals with clear ways to monitor them will assist you in preventing this avoidance. When done in the way I will outline in this chapter, goal setting can unlock amazing mind-sets—and results.

The human mind functions at its peak when it is receiving feedback. It's how we learn. We try things, watch what happens when we do, and then gauge what we should do next. There is mounting evidence that we can control heart rate and many other biometrics with feedback and practice.[2]

It's just as true in a baseball setting as it is in an office. When a major league baseball player gets three straight fastballs at exactly the same speed and in the exact same location and fouls them off, he's likely to be right on the fourth one because he's gotten feedback on his slight misses. The best hitters get better at getting hits against an opposing pitcher because they are adjusting the goals of their approach slightly with each at-bat. By the third or fourth they have gotten enough feedback to adjust and are more likely to get a hit.

Our brains are built to seek out new information and learn from the outside environment. The fact that you bought this book is proof of that on a small scale. A fully functioning human brain is always looking for ways to consolidate and make more efficient the process of acquiring new skills and information. The best way to create those shortcuts is to have a sort of mental road map to gain mastery in the area you are working on.

Goal setting is the process of creating that road map. I call it the Mastery Map.

The more specific and detailed a map you create, the more efficient and clear your feedback loop will be. You'll be able to tune in very finely to the details of a particular task and why it worked or didn't work. And you'll get much better much faster—getting to where you want to go with fewer missteps and wrong turns. Think of it as your success GPS: the more recent the download and the stronger network connection you have to your goal-setting program, the more likely—and more quickly—you are to get to your destination of mastery.

For example, say an NFL coach wants his quarterback to have a pass completion average of 60 percent. The quarterback currently completes about 55 percent of his passes, so he needs to improve his ratio by five percentage points, or about 10 percent.

There are many independent factors the quarterback could improve to bring up that percentage—everything from throwing mechanics to reading the defense more quickly to making better decisions with the ball. The coach could walk into a meeting and tell the quarterback simply, "You need to complete more passes" and leave that statement to the quarterback to try to reach that goal through trial and error.

Or the coach and player could sit together and come up with a set of short- and long-term goals that together would have the desired effect—attend three extra passing workouts per week to build more familiarity with the offense or improve defensive recognition to eight out of ten plays during film study. If the coach was one of the new breed who is more sophisticated in the realm of performance psychology, he might suggest that the player work on being more present in the moment during the game by working on his breathing.

The quarterback in the first example might get to 60 percent, but it would be based on luck, athleticism, or some other confluence of factors that are hard to measure and repeat. Even if he were successful, he wouldn't know why and wouldn't be confident that the results wouldn't disappear just as mysteriously as they appeared. In contrast, in the second case the quarterback would have a very clear road map to success—and plenty of indicators along the way showing why progress was being made or why it wasn't.

Two of the huge advantages to creating a Mastery Map are that it gives you an orderly idea of exactly what you need to improve in order to reach the goal, and it identifies potential roadblocks you could face and then gives you time to think about how you will deal with them.

We're actually set up from birth to build Mastery Maps. Your parents established the first performance feedback loops for you, perhaps by rewarding you for good behavior and punishing you for bad behavior. Then, when you enter the world of education, you learn very quickly which skills and habits result in good grades and which produce bad grades. But then, in the workplace and on our own, the goals and feedback can become very subjective. Your boss, coworkers, or friends might have clear ideas of what they want in terms of results, but they probably do not do a good job communicating these to you. Or maybe they do a good job communicating them, but those goals don't match the goals you have for yourself.

Even with the best boss in the best organization, it's sometimes hard to figure out what kinds of skills and behaviors will help you both identify productive goals and figure out what skills and behaviors will get you to those goals. By using the skills in this chapter, you'll be able to do just that by directing your attention in the right way—a kind of organizing principle for your mind.

Think back to the baseball player we talked about at the beginning of the chapter, the one who saw his name up on the scoreboard. If he just walked up to the batter's box each time angry and embarrassed about his stats and hoped he'd do better the next time, he'd have a hard time being focused on the small things that go into a productive at-bat—and he'd have an extreme amount of stress. But with good goal setting, he can go through his particular process and judge himself about how he kept oriented to that process, not whether or not he got a hit. The goal itself actually orients him to behavior that will make it more likely that he will be successful.

The other piece of the goal-setting alchemy is motivation. Motivation is a catchword in both the sports and business worlds because it represents such a strong emotional force. An athlete goes through a particularly tough period or suffers a bad injury, and you hear about how the experience has motivated him or her to work hard to get back. A couple wants to sell their house because they've already signed a contract for a new one, so you read in the listing that they're "motivated sellers."

They want to get it done.

When you build a set of goals that are firmly connected to your own internal sense of motivation, your "Power Value," as we'll discuss in Chapter 3, you have a built-in source of fuel to achieve those goals. When you come up with your own set of goals that would give you satisfaction if you achieved them, you're going to pay more attention and work harder than you would if you were shooting for goals that somebody else assigned you. You have a true investment in the outcome vs. following a script.

I've had countless conversations with baseball players in spring training, when many of them have been meeting with coaches to talk about the upcoming season. Those coaches have jobs to do, so they're certainly actively establishing things they want each player on the roster to work on for the season. It's a professional's job to work within that coaching structure and work on improving those skills, but I can tell you that from my vantage point, I can see a real, predictable difference between the goals a player buys into for himself vs. the ones that he doesn't connect with as well. The best coaches—and the best players—are able to create an environment where everybody works together to establish a productive set of short- and long-term goals and then do the big and little things to support the achievement of those goals. After you build your Mastery Map, it will help you to come back to it and rework the motivation section once you have read the chapter on motivation.

How Hard Is Too Hard?

Now that you're on board with setting process-oriented goals, how high exactly should you set the bar, so to speak? One of the most common snags people who set goals run into is that they set goals that are so far outside their normal behavior that they have set themselves up to fail—and when they do, the failure demoralizes them and influences them to stop trying. As researchers Gary P. Latham and Edwin A. Locke found, basing self-esteem purely on goal attainment distorts the reality of the situation.[3]

For example, if you're a baseball player coming into the major leagues for your rookie season, you could set a goal of hitting .320 and knocking in 150 runs, but those are extremely high bars. Those goals don't leave much room if you're hitting .280 and are sitting on forty RBIs at the midway point of the season. What's worse, if you fall short of your original far-fetched numbers, you may be so discouraged in the process that you underperform even more!

Ideal goals are the right combination of available and stretch. They should be ones you can achieve if you perform well but not so challenging that you have only a one-in-one-hundred chance for success.[4]

Take the example of the trader we talked about a few pages ago. If he set for himself a goal of improving his subjective calmness score by 50 percent, it would be far more effective for him to build steps into that process that broke the goal down into manageable pieces. If he simply said to himself, "Tomorrow I'm going to be 50 percent more calm," he would be setting himself up for frustration and disappointment—and he'd quickly abandon both the goal and the process of improvement.

A far more effective approach would be to find a level of improvement that is challenging but not overwhelming. That might mean shooting for 10 percent improvement over a week of trading sessions, and then another 10 percent improvement the following week, until the overall numeral goal was reached.

With objective goals the process is pretty straightforward. Maybe you've decided to get in better shape, and your process goal is to reach a certain average heart rate during thirty minutes of exercise per day. You could measure all of the average heart rates you achieve over the course of a week, then target the second or third best one as the average score you want to reach.

When you're talking about something subjective and self-assessed like "calmness," it can be a tricky job coming up with those benchmarks, especially when compared to something straightforward and objective like heart rate or calories consumed. One strategy I like to use for some of those harder-to-define subjective goals is to measure performance on the desired scale for a period of time, then establish as the goal the higher end of your measured ability. If the trader rated himself for calmness on a day-to-day basis and saw that his results ranged from 5 to 8 out of 10, he could reasonably establish as a preliminary goal an average score of 7.5 over the course of a week—essentially adding some objective measurement to a subjective score. Say your goal for the next three months is to have better communication with your supervisor. You could rate the quality of each communication on that same 0-to-10 scale and then target your next communications to be a rating of 7 or better.

Let me give you an example of what this looks like in the real world.

I was working with a woman who recently got promoted from COO to CEO at her real estate firm, and she said that one of her biggest challenges was feeling a lot of resistance from her team in her new role. She said she felt disconnected from some of the key executive staff and other important managing directors of her company. I told her it was natural to feel stress after taking a new role, and I asked her what specifically she wanted to change.

"I just wish they would give me a shot—that they would be more open to me as a leader and be able to see what I can do before they made judgments about me," she said. "Also I'd like to be more included in their conversations about their visions for the company because I think it'll help me to come up with ideas that will move this place forward."

I asked her whether she thought those goals were more outcome-based or based on how she acted or thought in a given situation.

"I guess a lot of that stuff is really out of my control and depends on what they think and what they do," she said.

I asked her what kinds of behaviors she could add or change to directly impact the situations causing her stress.

"Well, I think a lot of it has to do with the things I avoid or don't avoid," she said. "If I can come up with a few ways to join in with them and increase the positive conversations I have, I think that might lead to forming better relationships."

After a few coaching sessions the CEO went back and created a weekly lunch for the entire senior staff, at which she asked them not about work but about their lives outside the office. She also decided that she would make a regular sweep of the office—going door to door through the management suite each week, making conversation with everyone from the receptionist to senior leadership. Her goal was to show her colleagues that she was open and accessible for whatever concerns they might have.

Every week she would review her progress with both me and a friend who worked in a similar capacity at a different company. We focused only on how well she did in these conversations and on ways to improve her social interactions. During each coaching session we talked a lot about what her most enjoyable experiences were during the process—laughing over awkward exchanges when she tried to talk about topics outside her expertise (like hip-hop music) or where she confused people's names. We celebrated moments like the one when an up-and-comer from the marketing department who had previously been closed off seemed to open up after the woman's second sweep of that floor.

By focusing all of her goal setting on elements within her control, the CEO was doing the same thing my baseball clients do when they redefine pitching as a sophisticated game of catch or hitting as measuring preparedness and process. They turn the process into the goal and measure themselves by that yardstick.

Short-Term vs. Long-Term Goals

Page through a basic self-help book, and you'll see chapters and chapters devoted to building short-term and long-term goals. They'll go down to the grittiest detail, providing a very specific timeline cutoff for what constitutes short term vs. long term and how many of each you should have.

To me, making those kinds of very specific distinctions isn't as important as understanding an overall framework that makes the entire process work as seamlessly as possible for you.

There's no question that "segmenting," or breaking a big goal into manageable pieces, is a sound strategy for anybody. Your overall goal might be to make a successful presentation at an annual meeting at the end of this year. A real, first-level step toward achieving that goal might be to go through a practice session this week in which you focus on making eye contact within your five-person project team. When you "win" that small step of making eye contact in that setting, you're building your confidence and perpetuating the mind-set that you're in control of your progress.

At the same time, the bigger, long-term goal exists out there in the distance as the ultimate motivating factor behind making all of these small-scale moves and decisions day-by-day. Staying late after a game to take one hundred extra cuts in the batting cage might not be inspiring for a baseball player by itself, but when the player sees those extra cuts as a part of a bigger, more "noble" goal, like never going into a game without a full scouting report on the next opposing pitcher and a game plan for attack, it's easier to find the fuel so crucial for fighting through very human conditions like boredom, discouragement, and even laziness. Making those small, positive steps toward intermediate goals—and seeing how they create momentum toward a bigger, reachable goal—generates more momentum and energy to achieve those goals.[5]

Judgment: The Kryptonite of All Goals

"A winner is just a loser who tried one more time," said George M. Moore Jr., a war veteran who overcame devastating injuries sustained in battle.

He was onto something.

One of the biggest risks that comes with being unsuccessful in reaching a goal is giving up. Think of it in terms of the things that stop you from being consistent in working out. My gym routine usually falters because I've been sick for a few days or because I've gone on vacation. Once I go off track or break my "rule," it's easier to give up or let this break extend into two weeks or a month.

One way to explore this is to explore a strategy borrowed from the field of addiction called "relapse prevention." In addiction treatment, when someone has successfully changed a behavior (e.g., drinking less, quitting smoking, eating healthier, or curbing gambling) and then have a lapse, they are much more likely to relapse. Studies show, for example, that when smokers haven't smoked for a month and then, as a reward for "good behavior," have a single cigarette, they return to smoking.[6]

This idea is called the "abstinence violation effect," more commonly referred to as the "Oh, screw it effect."[7] Perhaps a more common example is what I refer to as the "three-cookie trap," where you decide to eat one cookie, but when you notice only two left in the row, you think, "Well, I've already eaten one—might as well just kill this row."

This is exactly the type of thinking we try to eliminate in building successful routines. To block the "three-cookie trap" in sports, we build reminders into routines that help athletes remember that just because they gave up a hit or an error, that doesn't mean they can't restart their routine and path toward a successful process at any time after their mistake. We all slip and eat a cookie, but with awareness and practice, we can avoid eating three!

Athletes have unwanted results in their performance all the time. They may strike out, give up a home run, or blow a game entirely. This can be dangerous to goal setting because if they give up on their goal, they allow this bad result to start an abstinence violation effect (or three-cookie effect!). In my experience the most toxic threat to achieving your goal is your response to obtaining a disappointing result or having your initial plan fail.

You are definitely more likely to reach your goal if you never give up. This has been true in the case of the most successful athletes in history. They find ways to stick to their goals even when they have setbacks on the path to their goal. Or even the perception that your goal wasn't reached. The famous myth of Michael Jordan involves him "being cut" from his varsity basketball team. In reality most accounts point to the fact that he was held in junior varsity for an extra year to give him more playing time and that the varsity coach needed a taller player at the time. But the reality doesn't matter as much as Jordan's reality. He was denied the chance to reach his goal, but he kept on playing until he reached the highest pinnacle of the sport.[8] This story brings new life to his much-cited quote about responding to failure on the path to achieving your goals: "I've missed over 9,000 shots in my career. I've lost almost 300 games. 26 times I've been trusted to take the game-winning shot and missed. I've failed over and over and over again in my life. And that is why I succeed."[9]

An enormous part of the journey to success in baseball—and in life—is dealing with experiences of perceived or real failure. Or simply less than ideal results. Again it comes down to the now-infamous process-versus-outcome question: Are we putting too much at stake into our success (*outcome*) and forgetting that part of getting there involves moments when we don't do a perfect job at whatever it is we're trying to do (*process*)? The road to success can't be expected to be a straight line if it's a big, important goal we're working on—it will be zigzagged and sometimes full of roadblocks and moments that make us feel like we have failed at it all. However, if we are able to step back and look at the bigger picture, we see that failures are in fact an inevitable and important *part* of a whole.

Besides those moments when we let the ball drop—no pun intended—or make avoidable mistakes, it's crucial to remember the endless slew of *random* unwanted results that can trip us up during our journey—the true uncontrollables. With so much randomness that can affect outcomes, we can get into trouble if we allow these mishaps and errors to seep in and affect our mind-set. They can quickly grow into huge failure monsters that point out everything we're doing wrong and actually impede our abilities to move forward and achieve our goals.

In baseball, if you are tremendously successful as a hitter about 70 percent of the time, that means that we still don't get the results we want, so it may become easy to be down about the small percentage of those "wanted" outcomes. The most successful people—or simply those playing life as sport—are able to adjust in the face of failure. They find a way to still battle toward their goals in the wake of unwanted results. Baseball, for example, is a game of inches—two inches to the left and it's a home run; two to the right, and it's a foul ball; two inches high, it's a ball and you lose the game; two inches lower and it's a strike winning you the World Series. It becomes about your ability to respond well when challenges come up or when things don't go your way. The most successful people in the game of life are the ones who are able to "fail better." They've gotten failing down to a science—and they utilize these moments to inspire and move them forward instead of getting stuck. They respond quickly and are able to rebound in the face of struggles. They learn to be okay with coming face-to-face with negative results and continuing to persevere not only in spite of but also due to these moments that don't initially feel very good. When it's not working out in one position, they move over an inch or two. The idea is for you to get comfortable with moving on however many inches and however many times it will take for you to catch the ball or hit your home run. You can become more comfortable with the "okayness" of having to adjust instead of allowing your brain to get foggy with the you-messed-ups. Let's look at an example.

When you think of the most iconic baseball player, which player over the last hundred years made the biggest impact? I'm referring to a guy who epitomizes what it means to be a star baseball athlete. Babe Ruth. In your vision of Ruth he's probably launching a ball off his bat into the stratosphere. However, you might be surprised to discover that this iconic power hitter actually started his career as a pitcher. Legend has it that there was a game during which his frustrations led him to throw a punch at the umpire, who had called "ball" on four of his consecutive pitches. He wasn't thrilled with the fact that he was playing only every four or five days, so he decided to fight for an outfielder position—a risk that could have played out very differently. The takeaway point is that upon feeling that pitching wasn't working out, he took that risk and adjusted—and made this rather big goal adjustment—in order to achieve whatever inner goal he had been seeking when it came to playing baseball. Needless to say, the image of Babe Ruth slamming home runs is indelibly burned into our memories, while the memory of his process—and sticking with his desire for success—is not something we readily consider an important part of his success.

This anecdote allows us to increase our awareness and sensitivity to the reality of goal achievement: that even the best of the best can fall short. Although we easily remember the score of the final game, the crowd cheering, tears streaming down their faces, we forget all of the missed shots or outs or serves into the net that got us here. These reminders help bring us down to earth and soothe our spirits when we feel like we're failing. They make the idea of the zigzag road or the mountain climb to goal achievement a little less scary. Famous author Samuel Beckett once wrote, "Ever tried. Ever Failed. No matter. Try Again. Fail again. Fail better." We can use this opportunity to shift perspective: okay, so this week we told ourselves we would go to the gym five times, but we went only once—for ten minutes. Instead of harping on this perceived failure to commit or beating yourself up for your lack of motivation, use this moment to shine: next week, fail a little better.

Most people judge themselves or react negatively to others' judgments when they fail to achieve their desired results. With rare exceptions, the high-achieving athletes and business people I have helped know how they will react to a negative result before it happens. They anticipate material and emotional issues that may interfere with their goal-setting success and know how they will react and how they will lean on others for support. These procedures will dovetail with the routines you design in Chapter 7.

It is essential to have "flushing" or "resetting" routines to help you move on from micro-failures—unwanted results that aren't career ending, like giving up a game-tying home run or failing to convert on a run-of-the-mill sales lead. The goal-setting map you will create will have a place to think about these obstacles and will remind you to build a way to avoid judgment and, thus, the abstinence violation effect. Having the self-talk and routines to move on from judging yourself is half the battle in doing what is necessary to achieve your goal when you fail: try again. It is your ability to work on your goals and adjust to adversity that allows you a path to success. As the famed basketball coach John Wooden said, "Failure isn't fatal, but failure to change might be."

Keeping Track

For any kind of road map to be effective, you have to know where you stand and where you want to go. Goal setting at its best is the creation of a mental and physical plan for that journey. So it stands to reason that you need an accurate, efficient way to both determine your starting point and measure your progress.

Part of that is developing the objective and subjective standards we talked about earlier—like the enjoyment scale or the targeted average of your heart rate. But beyond that, it's crucial to create ahead of time a written set of standards to which you can hold yourself through this process.

If you get up one morning and decide that you need to lose weight, you could have a five-minute conversation with yourself and establish that you need to eat better and go to the gym more often. But when you do it that way, you aren't establishing a clear set of process steps that you will take to make productive steps toward the goal, and you're giving yourself plenty of wiggle room within the vagueness of that one-sided conversation. How many times have you made one of those mental promises to yourself, only to say a few days later, "Okay, I'm going to commit to it tomorrow" or something to that effect?

Stacks of research support the ritual of clearly articulating your goals and writing them out so that you have a visual reminder. Putting goals on paper serves as a more serious kind of commitment to the process, and it makes it more clear to you and anybody else involved what you're trying to do and how you will accomplish it.[10]

Monitoring and measuring your goal makes the goal tangible, not just a wish. It establishes accountability. Many people report a struggle in being able to commit to their goal. The main reason this is the case is due to the fact that we naturally want to avoid (a) things that are hard and (b) things that may expose the fact that we may not be as good at something as we hoped or thought we would be. One of the greatest challenges to overcome in goal setting is the fact that we can easily get tired, overwhelmed, stressed, or bored of our particular goal and lose sight of why we are trying to achieve it. This can cause us to give up on our goal.

Let's look at another real-life example.

For one of my baseball clients, his outcome goal was very straightforward: to improve his batting average by getting more hits.

By making some adjustments to his goal-setting process, we changed that goal to increasing the quality of his at-bats by getting better at picking a good pitch to hit. We both agreed that if he could pick better pitches, he would be much more likely to achieve the outcome he wanted—namely, a higher batting average.

We created a set of preliminary goals based on how well he developed his skills in some of the basic areas we've talked about in this book—controlling his arousal level (Chapter 4) and visualizing certain sequences of pitches (Chapter 5). We also worked with the team's hitting coach to come up with a plan for making adjustments to his swing that fit with his batting average goal. Instead of levering up to try to power balls into "moon shots" out of the park, he worked on making a more consistent, level swing for square bat-ball contact.

To monitor his progress, we got together weekly to discuss some of the more subjective goals, and we also had a regular meeting with a hitting coach to get an evaluation on how well he was improving his pitch recognition and selection during games. We checked the statistics to see how many pitches he was seeing from each pitcher—a sign of selectivity—and how fast the ball was traveling off his bat when he made contact, which is a sign of how solidly he hit the ball regardless of whether he made an out.

After a few weeks of this process the hitter's batting average had jumped dramatically.

"Ever since I started focusing on things I could control, I feel so much more relaxed up there," he said. "I'm not pressing like I was. I used to get up there and think 'I gotta get a hit, I gotta get a hit.' Now I just think about breathing correctly and visualizing different pitches coming. It's weird how I just changed what I was aiming for, and it ended up with me getting the results I wanted."

That's a dynamic you can create for yourself as well. By identifying specifically what you want to change, why you want to change it, and how you can control your related thoughts and actions, you will be well on your way to success. Now I'll show you how to build your Mastery Map to get there.

Exercise:
The Mastery Map

We've spent some time talking about how goal setting is a figurative road map to success. You can build a literal road map too, your customized Mastery Map. It's something I do with my clients. It's a simplified flowchart that defines the goal you've set for yourself, and it outlines both the steps you need to take toward the goal and the potential roadblocks that could prevent you from getting there.

The exercise of drawing out your own Mastery Map might remind you of being in school, but in my experience the simple act of sketching it out over the course of ten or fifteen minutes has had a transformative effect on many of my clients.

A sample Mastery Map looks something like this:

MASTERY MAP

★ YOUR GOAL! ★

HOW WILL YOU MEASURE SUCCESS?

WHO WILL SUPPORT YOU?

FIND YOUR
ENJOYMENT

CHALLENGES?

HOW WILL YOU GET THERE?

WHAT IS YOUR PROCESS GOAL?

WHAT IS YOUR MOTIVATION? WHAT IS YOUR POWER VALUE?

★ WHAT IS YOUR OUTCOME GOAL? ★

© Jonathan Fader

Most of it is very self-explanatory.

At the top of the map, write down your ultimate goal. Maybe it's to lose thirty pounds or to get onto the ballot for your local school board election twelve months from now.

At the bottom of the map rewrite this outcome goal. In the next slot, directly above it, write down a sentence or two describing your motivation, or Power Value (which you will be even more familiar with after reading Chapter 3), for that goal. For weight loss, your motivation might be to be able to be more active with your kids. If you are trying to start a new business venture, perhaps your goal is to feel more independent and increase your enjoyment by having more freedom. You will have a deeper appreciation for how to fill in your power value once you have read the next chapter on motivation.

Above your motivation is the largest box in which to write. It is the description of what process goal or goals you will set to create success. These are the series of small-scale, building-block actions and thoughts that will actually contribute to achieving the overall goal. If you're trying to lose those thirty pounds, your process goals would be to change your diet and modify your level of physical activity. In this box and the following one you can write down the actions and thoughts you have control over that, when you improve them, will lead to success in your outcome goal.

The next three pieces of the chart put into writing—and into "real life"—exactly what your roadblocks might be, who you will look to for support, and how you will measure your success. Identifying the potential roadblocks directs your mind to work toward coming up with ways to overcome those barriers if and when you get to them. Establishing an "accountability representative" gives you an external check on your progress and provides one more piece of fuel to toss onto the motivational fire.

In addition to your own desire to be successful, you're adding in the desire to show progress to your trusted accountability partner. Give that person a copy of the map when you're done so that they can follow along and offer reminders and pep talks along the way. It is also important to ask them for the specific help you are looking for from them. Should they text you daily to check in, or just give you encouragement? The more you can do to plan responses that stave off the aforementioned abstinence violation effect or the feeling of giving up when there are some setbacks, the better you will get at overcoming small failures on your way to achieving your goal.

One of the most important—if not the most important—elements to the map is the thoughts in the mountain climber's head, which refer to finding your enjoyment. Let's be real here: if you establish a variety of goals that offer nothing but punishment and misery along the way, you might have some kind of narrowly defined "success," but it won't be sustainable in the long term. Goal setting is much more energizing and productive when you can find the facet of the process that you truly enjoy.

One thing that makes professional athletes different and separates them from "normal people" is that they have a fierce commitment to their goals. From the outside you may think it's because they are paid millions of dollars to perform, but in my experience it happens because they practice recognizing and embracing motivation and enjoyment in their goal-setting and attainment process.

When you focus on your motivation and enjoyment, each goal setting target can act as a self-reinforcing loop that produces more and more energy toward achieving the goal. Enjoyment requires practice. Ask yourself what you enjoyed about filling out the Mastery Map. What did it feel like to complete it? What are you most excited about in putting it in practice? What do you enjoy most about improving your mastery in this area of your life?

The more you can look around and take in the view as you're trying to climb, the better satisfaction you will have in the process, and more often than not, you'll climb higher. In order to clarify the way in which the mastery map is used for various goals, we have included three different examples: a sport situation, a business situation, and a fitness situation.

You will note that some of the strategies named in the example Mastery Maps (e.g., Visualization, Self-Talk, and Breathing) have not yet been introduced. You will learn more about them and how to apply them to your map and your overall plan to live life as sport in the coming chapters.

Enjoyment Exercise

When you've finished filling out your Mastery Map, give yourself a reward. Make sure to actually reward yourself right after finishing if you can—for instance, eat something delicious, get a massage, or indulge in an episode of your favorite TV show. What did you enjoy the most about the reward? Take a minute to really think about it.

MASTERY MAP

★ YOUR GOAL! ★

FIND YOUR **ENJOYMENT**

HOW WILL YOU MEASURE SUCCESS?
Refocus my measurements away from my batting average and onto number of pitches seen; hard hit balls; subjective evaluation of my at bat quality (0-100%).

WHO WILL SUPPORT YOU?
Discussing with my girlfriend, my coach, weekly conversation regarding quality at bats with my coach, talking to my girlfriend about how I've dealt with unwanted results.

CHALLENGES?
A slump; will overcome by reviewing this sheet and discussing with coach.

HOW WILL YOU GET THERE?
Improving my breathing in the batter's box; being diligent about my pre-performance routine (timing pitches while I'm on the on-deck circle) and visualizing; replacing negative self-talk with positive self-talk when encountering unwanted result.

WHAT IS YOUR PROCESS GOAL?
To increase the percentage of quality at bats (seeing more pitches, making more contact, swinging at more good pitches).

WHAT IS YOUR MOTIVATION? WHAT IS YOUR POWER VALUE?
To fulfill my true potential for achievement to set an example of perseverance for younger players.

★ **WHAT IS YOUR OUTCOME GOAL?** ★
Higher batting average.

© Jonathan Fader

MASTERY MAP

★ YOUR GOAL! ★

HOW WILL YOU MEASURE SUCCESS?

Consistency in routines,
subjective quality of the routines.

WHO WILL SUPPORT YOU?

Coworker on my team.

FIND YOUR
ENJOYMENT

CHALLENGES?

Tough client questions; distracted clients; physical anxiety
during presentation; USE ADAPTIVE SELF-TALK.

HOW WILL YOU GET THERE?

Visualizing peak performance; centering breath (See chapters 4 & 5).

WHAT IS YOUR PROCESS GOAL?

Maintain calm, confident demeanor before, during, and after presentation.

WHAT IS YOUR MOTIVATION? WHAT IS YOUR POWER VALUE?

Making my mark on the industry—Achievement/Power.

★ **WHAT IS YOUR OUTCOME GOAL?** ★

Make a successful presentation to a potential client.

© Jonathan Fader

MASTERY MAP

★ YOUR GOAL! ★

FIND YOUR
ENJOYMENT

HOW WILL YOU MEASURE SUCCESS?
Refocus my measurements away from
the number on the scale and toward
my enjoyment of physical activity.
Percent of gym attendance.

WHO WILL SUPPORT YOU?
My wife and my friend who is also trying to
lose weight. Review this sheet with them monthly.

CHALLENGES?
Sugar cravings; frustrations with not losing
weight "fast enough." Use resetting routine.

HOW WILL YOU GET THERE?
Using FitBit with my wife and friends to have accountability
and healthy competition; being active with my kids; taking
dance classes. Focus on adaptive self-talk mantras.

WHAT IS YOUR PROCESS GOAL?
To make the process of losing weight more enjoyable;
to focus on consistency at the gym.

WHAT IS YOUR MOTIVATION? WHAT IS YOUR POWER VALUE?
To create a healthier lifestyle for myself and reduce my current risk
for developing diabetes, so that I can live longer for my children.

★ WHAT IS YOUR OUTCOME GOAL? ★
Lose 20 pounds.

© Jonathan Fader

3

Motivation

When you're working with professional athletes who are in the middle of a deep slump, it's an intense experience. You're talking about their livelihood, and depending on where they are in their career, they can be thinking about a variety of things:

Am I going to make it?

Is this the end for me?

What if I'm not really that good?

What if I can't get out of this slump?

To break through some of that stress and anxiety, I usually start with what, on the surface, seems like a simple question:

Why do you want to succeed?

What usually follows is a confused silence, and then this:
"What do you mean, why? Who cares? I haven't had a hit in two weeks. That's what I'm trying to figure out."

But I'll keep pushing them for an answer.

Eventually they'll start to think back to when they were little kids and first had the idea that they wanted to make it to the big leagues. Astonishingly, virtually every player in every sport basically says the same thing at that moment. They all had the dream of making it with the best.

But that answer isn't the end of the discussion. Wanting to make it to the big leagues doesn't tell me—or them—anything meaningful about what drives them. When you think about it, the response is generic because it doesn't tap into any in-depth description of their motivation. There is no connection to their core values or underlying, intrinsic motives in that stock answer. So I'll keep asking the same question: Why?

Why do you want to be in the big leagues?

At this point most of the players aren't quite sure what I want to hear, so they fall back onto their default answers.

Money

Winning

Fame

Those aren't *wrong* answers. They're just not usually the *truest* answer. "What will those things bring to you or your life? What will it feel like to get there? What do you mean, 'It will feel great?'" I'll ask. With some pushing and prodding, we get to the heart of it. One player told me he played to honor his father, who was a terrific player himself but sacrificed everything to provide his son with the chance to play. Another player told me that performing well on the field was the one time he felt truly fulfilled in his life—either on the field or off—and he wanted to extend that experience for as long as possible. Another said that he had a burning desire to prove wrong all of the people who doubted him.

As I said before, none of these answers are right or wrong. What makes these answers special is that they are unique and specific motivations that are more connected to the intrinsic feeling and drives of the individual athlete. They aren't pulled from the default grab bag of responses but instead give a genuine picture of what fuels their fire. How does this relate to you?

You have your own motivations for what you do. Those underlying forces are examples of what I call "Power Values"—core principles that make up who you are and, in most cases, are the "gas" that, when harnessed, can power you along the way toward success.

In many of these conversations I have with elite athletes I witness their very first time expressing that true motivation, which could only come from somewhere within the deepest parts of themselves. When the words come out I observe an amazingly clarifying experience. They're shocked by the sudden focus they feel toward their goal that is fueled by clarifying their Power Values.

Identifying these deep underlying values is what propels people to work hard and "reach down for a little something extra" as they strive for greatness. At the elite level—where everyone is talented—it can be the separating factor between a pitcher who can throw 98 miles per hour with intense focus at the beginning of a game and one who can do that in both the first inning and the seventh, when he's already thrown 101 other pitches. It can be the difference between being distracted by the inevitable nuisance injuries every player has in the playoffs at the end of a long season and playing as if you're as fresh as you were in the middle of an outstanding spring training.

Each individual moment of an athlete's career fits together along a string of different levels of motivation. Look closely at how intrinsically motivated they are, and you will find a spectrum of difference between a player who doesn't take advantage of his or her physical gifts and one who succeeds despite having less physical talent. I recently had the opportunity to take part in a 30 for 30 documentary, which was a collaboration between Marvel and ESPN. Entitled *Genesis*, the movie focused on the concept of how elite athletes are similar to superheros. Through interviewing some greats such as Russell Wilson, Cal Ripkin, Danica Patrick, Brandi Chastain, Colin Kaepernick, Carmelo Anthony, Henrik Lundqvist, Tony Hawk, Manny Pacquiao, Albert Pujols, and others, the project examined how and why these individuals emerged as success stories in the same way that a superhero would. Despite their immense talents, one unifying factor among these success stories was that they all "wanted it." They had a strong, almost insatiable desire to succeed from a young age. My belief and my comments, when I was interviewed in the documentary, are that each athlete, each person, is born with an innate ability. Think of it as hardware. And then you learn techniques and are exposed to teaching—call that software. You can have the best operating system, but if you don't use it well, you won't have the best results. Whether you are an elite athlete, a business person, or a parent, that is where motivation comes into play.

Strong, clear motivation can be the difference between winning and losing, both on the field and in life.

Identifying, clarifying, and using motivation don't happen by chance or magical thinking; they're a result of practicing a strategy that you will get familiar with in this chapter. Once you can identify that energy source of your Power Value, you'll be amazed at the level of intensity, focus, and determination you'll be able to tap into.

It appears that for humans the depth of the motivation well may be deeper than we think. We've all heard the anecdotal examples of people who find the ability to perform superhuman acts of "hysterical" strength when faced with the motivation of saving a human life. If you haven't, here they are:

In 1982 in Lawrenceville, Georgia, Angela Cavallo, lifted a car that had fallen on top of her son Tony high enough for two neighbors to pull Tony from beneath the car. In 2006 in Ivujivik, Quebec, Lydia Angiyou saved several children by fighting a polar bear. In 2006 in Tucson, Arizona, Tom Boyle lifted a Camaro off Kyle Holtrust while the driver of the car pulled the teen to safety. In 2009 in Ottawa, Kansas, Nick Harris lifted a Mercury sedan off a six-year-old girl pinned beneath. In 2011 in Tampa, Florida, University of South Florida college football player Danous Estenor lifted a 1990 Cadillac Seville off a man who had been pinned under the rear tire. In 2012 in Glen Allen, Virginia, twenty-two-year-old Lauren Kornacki rescued her father, Alec Kornacki, after the jack used to prop up his BMW slipped, pinning him under it. In 2013 in Oregon teenage sisters lifted a tractor to save their father, who was pinned underneath. In 2015 in St. John's, Newfoundland, Nick Williams lifted an SUV to save a young boy pinned underneath.[1]

These superheroic acts are thought to be fueled by adrenaline—but where does this adrenaline come from? A spark seems to be ignited when we see another human in danger. A similar spark or motivation can be present in other nonemergency life and sport activities as well. In particular, a powerful example of this extra "well" of motivation that we can all pull from comes from the world of extreme sports.

In the annual Race Across America cyclists test the limits of human endurance in a three-thousand-mile trek across the United States. The race takes place in June—in the heat of the summer—and requires riders to pedal as fast as they can from the West Coast to the East Coast, going dozens of hours at a time without any rest.

After days of grueling cycling, many of the riders start to lose control of their neck muscles and have to tape their helmets to the back of their seats to stay upright. Exhausted by the effort of pedaling and the lack of sleep, they often start to hallucinate that they are being chased by mythical creatures. Even in this dazed state the subconscious mind is *still* trying to help them to complete the goal because their motivation is so deep-seated, internal, and authentic.

One athlete who epitomizes this type of extreme endurance is the Slovenian cyclist Jure Robič. Robič is famous for thriving in races in which he routinely bests others while riding three thousand miles in eight grueling days, sleeping only ninety minutes a day. "Why do I do this?" he asks himself. "I find motivation everywhere. . . . Three years ago I got angry at the mountain. I climbed it 38 times in two months."

He also speaks openly about how his father neglected him while favoring his brother: "All my life I was pushed away. . . . I get the feeling that I'm not good enough to be the good one. And so now I am good at something, and I want revenge to prove to all the people who thought I was some kind of loser."

One idea as to how these athletes find this extra power is the concept of the "Central Governor." Scientists once thought that our muscles would just give out because of their physiological potential. Now there are theorists who think that the human body has a system, referred to as the Central Governor, that is responsible for protecting the body from overexertion.[2] Think of it as the small yellow light on your car that comes on when you have only thirty miles left of potential in your gas tank. You actually have some more reserves, but should probably stop so you don't run out of gas in the middle of the highway halfway between Los Angeles and Las Vegas!

Some say that our body functions in the same way. In other words, our body is telling us that the fact that we are exhausted and can go no more is merely a strong suggestion. Robič and other extreme athletes capitalize on this idea by ignoring their body signals and even welcoming the signs that their body has given up and that their mind is taking over. They make a decision to respond differently to these messages that tell them to give up and are instead using their inner Power Values as fuel. As Robič says about his desire to prove he is a winner to the ghosts of his father and brother, "These feelings are all the time present in me. They are where my power is coming from."[3]

The Building Blocks of Motivation

Scientists in the field of psychology have thoroughly studied human motivation. They have found that you can divide motivation into two broad categories: internal (intrinsic) motivation and external (extrinsic) motivation. One primary difference between these motivations is control. An internal motivation is one conceived and governed by you. An external motivation is one that comes from somebody else or from something else outside you (e.g., money). It's the difference between resolving to be the best you can be at something because it is of great personal importance to you for a specific reason and resolving to achieve a goal because of a concrete but meaningless reward.

An important scientific theory that has showcased the importance of intrinsic motivation is called the Self-Determination Theory, advanced by Edward Deci. This theory discusses how your perception of competence, relatedness, and autonomy are all important components of developing and sustaining intrinsic motivation.

In my career as a psychologist helping all kinds of people live life as a sport and perform at their best, the research and theories of Drs. William Miller and Stephen Rollnick have tremendously affected my work. Together these scientists developed an approach called Motivational Interviewing (MI).[4] MI has been shown to help people to find motivation even in extremely hard-to-change, addictive behaviors. Many theorists believe that MI helps people to change because it creates an autonomous place for people to identify and strengthen their own intrinsic or internal motivations.[5] At the end of this chapter you will learn an MI-based technique for identifying and sharpening your own intrinsic motivations. The more aware you are of your intrinsic motivations and the more you view your motivation as something you can develop, the easier it will be to put your Mastery Map into practice.

Strong internal motivations have been shown to positively affect outcomes in everything from sports to military settings. West Point researchers found that people who had internal motivation performed better than their classmates in many measures of academic and career success when compared to those with a mix of external and internal motivations.[6] More importantly, when people identified their internal and personal reasons related to their values and motivations, they were more likely to succeed in their goals.[7]

A person's level of internal motivation is a key difference between success and failure. Even if you have the built-in advantages—talent, speed, smarts, training—but no urge to push yourself to your limits and beyond, you're susceptible to being eclipsed by the person who has what psychologist Ellen Winner calls the "rage to master."[8] It happened to Georgetown in the NCAA tournament, and it happened when Ryan Leaf lost his starting position to Moses Moreno—a lightly regarded seventh-round draft pick. It happened when Muhammad Ali upset George Foreman for the Heavyweight Champion of the World in Zaire in the Rumble in the Jungle of 1974.

Your ability to refine and be aware of your specific motivation will help you perform at your best and maintain the energy and determination to sustain your hard work along the way to greatness. For instance, it could be understanding that your motivation to be a successful lawyer comes from seeing a loved one experience injustice, that your drive to be the best possible dad is motivated by wanting to make the world a kinder, more peaceful place, or that your need to be the best possible salesperson comes from the strong desire to model perseverance for your children—these examples demonstrate how critical intrinsic, deep-rooted motivations are to your stamina in pursuing a goal. Being able to sharpen your understanding of that motivation will allow you to keep working toward success. By using techniques that athletes use to understand and develop motivation, you can also harness and sustain that drive to improve and reach your own peak performance.

The process isn't quite as simple as reading this chapter, setting the book down for a few minutes, and walking away with your brightly polished, shiny motivation in hand. The process is more akin to using a metal detector to find something valuable during a walk on the beach.

Sweeping the sand with the detector, it might take some walking to get to a place where the machine beeps to let you know something is under the sand. And when you do find something, you have to dig down and brush it off to see if you have a real treasure. Once you spend some time cleaning and polishing, you then learn whether you've got a rare coin (a Power Value) or just a scrap of metal.

This is the process for finding your motivation. At first you might not know exactly what your Power Value is. You might start out with superficial thoughts about your desire to perform well at work, in a relationship, or on the field. But as you dig down and polish, you'll see more and more.

It will take some effort.

Mike Richter, the NHL superstar goalie for the New York Rangers, was a decorated goaltender throughout his amateur hockey career, playing for the University of Wisconsin and the US National and Junior National teams in the Olympics and World Championships. By the time he made his NHL debut in 1989, during the New York Rangers' playoff run, he was one of hockey's brightest prospects.

Inside the cauldron that is the New York City sports and media scene, it would have been easy for Richter to become obsessed with a definition of "success" and "winning" that wasn't necessarily his own. But instead he decided he was going to hold himself to his own standard of greatness and used that personal barometer as motivational fuel.

"For me the goal was reaching my potential—whatever it was. It wasn't to be the best. It was to be *my* best," Richter told me during a lively conversation about what kept him motivated across many successful years as a hockey player. "The only person who can determine that is you. You know how much effort you put in, and you know how well you're focusing. From there all you can control is what you can control. How much focus are you bringing to the moment? How much positive energy are you bringing?"

When I asked him later about how much he was motivated by winning, he had a fascinating answer. "If you're motivated purely by wins and losses, that's very *binary*," Richter said. "Your happiness is then tied into many things over which you don't have control. What happens if you're playing against an obviously inferior opponent and you can win at half-speed. Is that really a 'victory'? And what if you play great, but the team doesn't win? Is that really a 'loss'? I was always motivated by winning the 'game within the game.' I wanted to be able to be in the moment, control what I could control, and bring my maximum effort. Win or lose, I wanted to be able to walk out of the arena feeling like I learned something and I got better."

Mike's Power Values were connected to effort and enjoyment, and he was quickly able to establish them as non-negotiable within his personal success-failure frame. "I'd come to practice and see somebody like defenseman Brian Leetch, and an hour before he'd be on the couch, exhausted. But for the forty-five minutes of skate around, he played as if it was the seventh game of the Stanley Cup finals," Richter told me with a big smile on his face. "And that's exactly it. Your habit needs to be that you go out there every time with a perfect mind-set and perfect approach. The good players? They say, 'I'm going out to play. I wouldn't go out there without my skates. I'm not going out there with that mind-set.'"

Like Richter, Juwan Howard was a highly recruited basketball players coming out of high school in Chicago. A talented, big man with a soft shooting touch, Howard was part of the Fab Five recruiting class of 1991 at the University of Michigan, and he went on to become an All-American center for the Wolverines. He played twenty seasons in the NBA, winning two titles and becoming the first man to sign a $100 million contract in basketball with the Washington Bullets in 1996. Despite leaving Michigan early for the NBA draft, Howard continued taking classes at night and in the offseason, and he earned his degree from Michigan in 1995. He and I had a conversation late one night that explored a continued thread stressing the importance of staying motivated and practicing enjoying what you do.

Plenty of players get to the top level of professional sports and "coast" as much as their talent will allow. It takes a special player to have both the talent and the motivation to get the most out of that talent. In our conversation that night, Juwan and I had an inspiring discussion about what motivated him in his successful career. "Being good at basketball isn't the same as having passion for the game," he told me with the intensity of a seasoned veteran. "Fader, when I was a young kid growing up, I was outside playing from sunup and sundown. I was tall for my age, so I was usually playing against people four or five years older. You didn't get on the court unless you had skills and toughness. That love and passion for the game drove me through all of those pickup games up through college and nineteen years in the NBA. Unless you have that passion, you're never going to get the most out of yourself."

Along with his internal motivation, Juwan was also very aware of how fortunate he was to get his NBA shot. "It's natural to get upset about the wins and losses and whether or not you played well," Juwan told me. "But I always tried to keep the right perspective and a positive approach, because I knew how lucky I was to be able to be in that moment." Juwan showed me how he used to stay motivated on tough days by reminding himself to be grateful for his experience: "How many people out there wish they had the opportunity to play just one game in the NBA? Maybe they got hurt or derailed some other way and never got to experience what I got to experience. I never wanted to waste my opportunity."

What Mike and Juwan understood so well was that it wasn't enough to feel a generic need to "work harder" or "practice more." Unless that need was connected to a clear, visceral reason or motivator, it wouldn't be nearly as effective.

For example, many people are on a constant self-improvement mission. It's why books like this one are published in so many numbers. Many of the motivations behind that self-improvement will probably sound very familiar to you. We all want to be happier, earn more money, and have better relationships. But those "wants" aren't nearly as sustaining as truly internal, precise motivating factors that make accomplishing that goal a *necessity*.

You can use the same technique yourself, right here, right now. In the space below write out an external goal you have in your professional life, such as accomplishing a particular sales goal for the quarter or finishing a certain complicated project:

Now, ask yourself a series of cascading "why" questions below that external goal:

Why do I want to . . .

Increase my sales 25 percent?

Improve my relationship?

Be a better parent?

Be more financially successful?

Improve my golf game?

Answer the question, and if the answer doesn't motivate you to put this book down and go do something toward achieving that goal, ask yourself the next questions:

Why did I answer what I did?

How would success in this area change my life for the better?

What is at stake for me if I fail to achieve this goal?

How would success in this area impact those I love?

When I achieve my goal, what will be the best part of my success?

Keep going until you get to a value, idea, or principle that inspires you to get up from the chair and take action. It might be something small at the beginning. That's perfectly okay. The most important thing is that you find that *internal* motivator that calls you to action. It could be tied to a specific belief or value you have related to your family, religion, or long-term dream.

I had a client who was a successful novelist. She was constantly suffering from the bane of all authors: the dreaded writer's block. Her production was as spotty as a streaky hitter in baseball. Some weeks she found herself producing forty pages a week, while other times ten days would go by and all she would see was the blinking vertical line of her cursor. We spent a whole meeting delving deeply into what really motivates her. Despite her deep philosophical bent and impressive educational pedigree, she pointed to some concrete reasons for writing her new book: "I'd like another bestseller."

When I asked the cascading questions from above, our conversations yielded some more powerful answers. She told me that the reviews for her last book questioned her talent. They criticized her, suggested that her first book was perhaps a "fluke" and that she might not be able to write in the way she had before. She talked to me about her desire to show not only them but also herself that the voice inside her was "still alive."

When I asked her why it was important to show that this talent was still strong, I expected her to focus on the desire to prove the critics wrong. But she surprised me. She told me that she had a history of depression that we never talked about before. In her youth, before she found writing, she struggled with sadness, and isolation. When she discovered writing as a twentysomething, it allowed her to create meaning in her life. Her desire to hold onto that meaning and the improvements writing made to her self-esteem, her marriage, and general well-being were strong Power Values. Becoming more aware of these values and reminding her of them would lead her to more consistent writing and several best-selling books in the years to come. At the end of this chapter I'll show you a more in-depth mechanism for identifying your own personal Power Value.

The Power of Accountability

There's a reason elite football wide receivers get together in the offseason to train in small groups. It's the same reason virtually every exercise guide starts with the advice that you'll get better results if you have a workout partner or a trainer you see on a regular basis. It's why the military trains its recruits in close-knit groups and professional sports teams bring everybody together for preseason training. And it's why the greatest sports and entertainment performances of all time have happened in front of thousands of cheering fans.

We're social creatures, so motivating ourselves in isolation is incredibly difficult. When you're trying to reach a goal or change a behavior, you need all the help you can get from the important people in your life to support and reinforce your journey. It's easy to identify these individuals—they are your partners, friends, family, coworkers. It's not always so easy to enlist the right kind of motivational help from your inner circle. Think of this motivation you're identifying and building inside you as a fire. Like any fire, it needs to be built and tended to, and if you don't pay attention and feed it with wood, it will go out. Choosing the right coaches to feed that fire, so to speak, is critically important.

This motivational caretaking is one of the main reasons you see so many coaching changes in professional sports. Even the most talented and knowledgeable coaches can lose that connection with their team, and the time comes to find somebody else who can rekindle the motivational fire.

I'm certainly not suggesting you should kick your husband or wife or coworker out of your inner circle! But the better job *you* do at managing these relationships in terms of what you need from your coach, the happier and healthier those relationships will be in the long term. Also, think carefully about who you pick to be involved in your goal. You might love your best friend to death, but there may be a coworker or other acquaintance who pushes you in a more effective way or who you just feel more comfortable being honest with about your goals and challenges.

To help identify the right coach in your life, you need to be upfront about what you're trying to do with your goals and motivation and be direct with the people in your circle. When you have a discussion with your partner about what you need, be specific. Do you want somebody to be an accountability partner, who checks in on you from time to time to make sure you aren't slacking? Is it somebody to give you periodic inspiration by reminding you of your Power Values from time to time? Or is it more of a hard-core participation partner who agrees to go to the gym with you three times a week so you can cheer each other on? Have a motivation conversation in which you are explicit about why you are attempting to achieve something—your Power Value—and what exactly you would like them to do.

It's crucial to come together on the frequency and form of communication between you and your coach to establish your motivation as a regular part of your life. Make sure you are clear about how accountability will help sustain your motivation when you fill out your Mastery Map from the goal-setting chapter (Chapter 2).

Motivation and Habits

We all have habits—good ones and bad ones. And most scientists agree that habits are learned and reinforced in a relatively straightforward way. We're cued by something in our environment and then we behave a certain way, and that behavior is reinforced by some kind of reward. For example, you might taste a certain kind of candy bar and think it's fantastic. Every time you see one of those bars, you tear it open and eat it. It has become a habit with a reward, even if the long-term effect of eating a bunch of chocolate isn't so great.[9]

In sports, athletes develop all kinds of good and bad habits as well. A pitcher might spend an hour after every start reviewing video of each hard-hit ball against him in order to see whether he hit or missed his location. That prep work leads him to feel more prepared for the next start and becomes an ingrained piece of his postgame ritual. Bad habits are easy to groove too. A hitter who has been struggling to turn on good fastballs might start "cheating" by guessing a fastball is coming and starting his swing earlier. If he hits a few good fastballs—reinforcing his behavior—he'll keep doing it. But pitchers will quickly catch on to this game and change speeds, making the batter look foolish when he swings way out in front.

Anybody who has tried to change a habit knows how hard they can be to break. That's why it's essential to build in the natural fuel of Power Values into the habit cycle to change that loop into something more productive. When you do that you're actually using the inborn mechanism of habit formation to hardwire motivation into your everyday experience.

For example, if your goal is to improve the process of your sales calls, achieving the goal needs to have a positive consequence in motivational terms—like a phone call to your coach to give him or her the thumbs up about your success. That motivational "win" serves to reinforce the usage of your Power Values in achieving goals and adds gasoline to the engine. In other words there has to be a reward in your habit loop to maintain any hard work you do in changing your routines or goal setting.

This was especially true with New York Mets outfielder Michael Cuddyer, who created a clever and inspirational exercise to motivate the rest of the team. He picked up an inexpensive, cheesy-looking wrestling championship belt and made a spectacle of gathering the team after a win and presenting the belt to the player who contributed the most to the victory.

This type of motivation is so powerful because it combines the intrinsic desire for recognition of ability and talent with the social reinforcement of your family or team. When asked what the impact of this type of motivation was, players and coaches both pointed to how enjoying the fun of the competition together fueled their performance.[10]

Motivation in the Wild

Concepts and theories are great, but what happens when you're out there in the field or in the office? It's easy to talk about motivation and values in the abstract and to write them down in a list. But what about when you're face-to-face with a situation that threatens to sink all of this newfound motivation and confidence you've been building?

First, it's time to accept something that might sound counterintuitive coming from a psychologist who is supposed to be eternally sensitive: feelings don't always matter. No, I'm not suggesting that it's okay to trample over your partner's or friend's feelings to get what you want. But inside your own mind it's time to let go of the distinctly modern idea that you need to feel

a certain way before you can act a certain way with any consistency. Actually, in many cases the reverse is usually true. Behavioral psychology has shown us that how you act triggers you to
feel a certain way. Why does this matter?[11]

Because even if you can't always control your emotions, you
can control your actions and thoughts associated with those actions. And if you can control your actions, it often leads to feeling differently. That means that believing you need to be
motivated before you can act is usually just a tactic that helps
you to avoid being uncomfortable. If you we tell ourselves that
we don't feel ready—we are too tired, scared, or sad to start a
behavior—we use this feeling to avoid the behavior that may
lead to success. In reality, even if you're not motivated, you
should act the way you would if you *were* motivated. Not only
will your feelings respond to those physical cues, but by placing
yourself in the moment and exposing yourself to possible enjoyment, you'll also experience a set of interactions with people
and things that may lead to finding that motivation more regularly. You'll be setting up the pathway to motivation, so to speak.

For example, you might get invited to a party and feel "unmotivated" to go. You might be feeling shy or lazy or insecure or
think that it won't be any fun because you won't have anybody
to talk to. But after some gentle prodding from a friend, you
grudgingly decide to go. More often than not, a half hour into
the party you find yourself chatting away, surprised at how
much you're enjoying yourself and motivated to get in there and
engage with people.

Finding that satisfaction at a party might seem like a small
thing, but it speaks to my greatest goal with this book: to offer
you ways to use sport psychology strategies to increase not only
your performance but also your *satisfaction* with that performance. I want you to have success, but just like the elite athletes

I work with, my goal is to assist you in enjoying the process of playing the sport of life.

Reality will certainly deal you some unpleasant hands from time to time, and how you motivate yourself to respond and even flourish during those situations will play a huge role in determining how much you can enjoy life from day-to-day, whether it's dealing with a person in your office you really dislike or finding the passion to perform in an environment that is truly toxic.

You can transform any moment in your day by changing the playing field and focusing on playfulness or enjoyment. One of our favorite games to play in my house involves actively trying to delay a person who's in a rush to get something done. On the surface that might not sound like such a nice thing to do, but hear me out!

When one of us is scurrying around, trying to get ready, one of the other people in the family will try to ask that person about something they truly love and engage them in a conversation about it. For example, if my wife is late, I might ask her about interior design or fashion as a way of playing this game. My wife might ask me about surfing or baseball. The goal is to prolong the person's dawdling by seeing if you can get them to engage in a conversation about this topic of interest—and slow down to savor quality interaction with a loved one. It's annoying as all get-out. But once the person realizes what's going on they usually laugh, and although still late, they are now engaging with the stress of life in a different way. I have extended this game to engaging with hostile people in stadiums, offices, and hospitals around the world. Get them talking about something they like and—voilà!—their personality begins to transform.

You can do the same thing with a disagreeable person outside the house. Make it a game to see what kind of conversation you engage in with them to help you become more interested in their story. How good can you get at eliciting a positive response from somebody who might otherwise be in a state of perpetual misery? The playfulness concept works along similar lines. Instead of focusing so hard on the stressful and anxiety-laden interactions that are a part of everyday life, create a game for yourself to see if you can make the next stranger you interact with in the workplace laugh. This enjoyment and playfulness and focus on action can help you jumpstart your motivation to go to a meeting, participate on a call, or spark the motivation to change a relationship with a difficult person. By practicing playfulness you can change your level of motivation for engaging in boring, annoying, stressful, or even hateful activities and situations.

On the baseball field this practice of playfulness translates well when dealing with motivation to play through one of the most dreaded situations: slumps. Many of the techniques introduced later in this book help with breaking out of slumps in every area of the sport of life. Still, the process of playing while you are obtaining less than ideal results can be painful at best and, at worst, can suck all the motivation out of the largest ballparks, meeting rooms, and sales calls. To spark motivation to stay in the game, I recommend playful practice to players in the same way I discussed above. For a struggling player I suggest things like being the first person in the dugout waiting for a high five when your teammate hits a home run. Making a wisecrack or joke to the reporter after you engage in the requisite discussion of how hard you are working to break out of the slump. By engaging in things that you do when playing well, your resulting feeling and attitude will be positive. This fosters motivation, and before you know it, you'll be hitting well again.

As you start to play these games with yourself, you'll essentially be developing a motivational "shorthand" that will help you snap back into place when you feel yourself losing some fuel. As I mentioned, with my clients I use the term "ME," where the M stands for *Motivation* and the E stands for *Enjoyment*. Before each important activity, meeting, or event, athletes I work with will go through a mental routine in which they remind themselves to "put the ME into it"—that is, clarify their motivation and keep it close to their consciousness and practice enjoyment.

How-To: Find Your Power Value

You can easily incorporate an exercise I use with athletes to help them identify what values and motivations are the most important to them. It is a variation of a powerful technique used in motivational psychology called the Value Card Sort, which is adapted from a motivational interviewing exercise.[12]

Take a look at the values listed on the attached pages. Decide which ones are the most important to you in relationship to the life goals you are working on. Once you've been able to pick three that are the most meaningful to you, cut them out and place them on a table.

These three core motivations are your *Power Values*.

Once you've identified these, ask yourself the following questions about how each of these values is related to your actual goal, like improving your overall fitness or achieving something at work or in your relationship:

How did you go about choosing the values that you chose?

What makes these values important to you?

When you look at the cards you picked, what do you make of them?

How does the issue you are trying to improve relate to the values you chose?

How did identifying these values affect you?

If you didn't make progress in your goal, how would that impact your value?

How would achieving the goal impact your life in relation to your Power Value?

As you draw a closer connection between the goal and those values, the values themselves will serve as a catalyst for the day-to-day groundwork you do to make the goal become a reality. You can think of the actual techniques you use to achieve the goal—say, meeting a trainer twice a week for the fitness goal—as the car, and then think of your Power Values as the gas that feeds the engine and makes it go.

In the world of elite sport this ability to identify and utilize Power Values is often what separates athletes who are able to sustain hard work toward a particular—usually lofty—goal and those who can't. When you have identified why this power value is important for the goal(s) you are working on, write the reason why it is important on the actual card for the value you selected.

To reinforce the power of the Power Values, you need to give them a prominent, visible place in your life. To do that, create a simple Power Value statement that you can print out and attach somewhere so you can see it during your day—such as the bottom edge of your computer screen or inside your locker at the gym. You can use the actual card that you cut out of this book. You can even make it the wallpaper on your cell phone's lock screen. Many athletes take the permanent step of tattooing some form of a Power Value statement right on their bodies. LeBron James famously has "Chosen 1" inked in giant letters across his back, and "No one can see through what I am except for the one who made me" on his right forearm. David Beckham's tattoos of his wife's name in Hindi characters and the flames that state "Let them hate as long as they fear" do a lot to help him focus on what motivates him.[13]

The purpose of the statement is to remind you of the specific and powerful reason you're engaging in all this hard work toward your goal.

For example, one player client wrote, "This one, for my father" on a piece of paper and taped it to the inside of his locker. It was a reminder of how he wanted to live every moment to the fullest and honor his dad by doing the things his father's situation prevented him from doing. Once you pick your Power Values and decide how they are connected to your goal, you can tape them up in a similar way on your desk, wall, or locker and benefit from their power in your performance in work or at home in the same way a professional athlete does in the middle of a long season. By doing this you will keep your fire alive to achieve your goal.

HEALTH

RELATIONSHIPS

ACHIEVEMENT

SELF-ESTEEM

POWER

INDEPENDENCE

PLEASURE

PASSION

✂

RESPONSIBILITY

COMPASSION

CREATIVITY

LOVE

PURPOSE

GENEROSITY

FAITH

STABILITY

© Jonathan Fader • www.jonathanfader.com

Enjoyment Exercise

When you're coming up with your motivations for accomplishing your goals and setting values to them, take a break and do an activity you enjoy that is already naturally fueled by intrinsic motivation (e.g., playing with your children, taking a hike, etc.). Ask yourself how this activity is connected to your Power Values. This will remind you of the powerful connection that your inner motivation can have on accomplishing any kind of task or activity. You will be able to enjoy a goal more readily if you've already found your motivation for it. Take a minute to really have an outside look at yourself enjoying the moment. Sit with the enjoyment for a bit.

4

Managing Anxiety

The video is hilarious—unless you're me.

It starts with me in the parking lot, raising my fists like I've just won the heavyweight championship of the world. You can hear the wind hard across the camera's microphone and see the tall grass in the open airfield behind me getting blown horizontal.

In the next scene I'm looking a little less confident as I'm getting strapped into some skydiving equipment. My eyes are darting around as the jump coordinator yanks hard on the parachute straps to make sure I'm secure.

Next I'm walking onto the tarmac toward the airplane. I've gone completely pale, as if the blood has drained from my body. My friend, who is filming, keeps trying to get me to respond to questions, but all I can manage is a weak smile and a half-hearted wave.

In the last shot I'm on the plane and we're in the air. I'm strapped to the jump coordinator, and the door to the plane slides open to reveal the blue sky. I turn to the camera to try to say something glib, but no words come out. I'm sweating, and I look like I'm about to throw up.

The sensations I experienced during my first skydive are the perfect example of "biological alarm." Our bodies are built with an automatic internal regulating system (the sympathetic nervous system) that works very much like a sensitive smoke detector. It's designed to go off if there's the slightest hint of a "fire," which, in evolutionary terms, is something that could cause physical harm. For our ancestors "fire" might have been a predator like a lion in close proximity, and the alarm system primed the body to go into red-alert mode—blood pumping extra oxygen to the brain and muscles to make fast decisions and quick movements. It prepared humans to either run away or confront an attack in the classic "fight or flight" response.

That alarm system has been our friend for thousands of years in the sense that it has helped our ancestors identify danger and is one of the main reasons we still exist as a species. After all, if we didn't have this alarm system, the lion would have eaten us—or our ancestors, that is! But there's one problem with it: it doesn't do a good job of separating real threats from perceived ones.

In many of the situations you might face on a playing field or in a conference room you're challenged by very real fear. But your body responds to that fear as it would if you were under physical attack, not in proportion to the size of the threat.

If you miss a free throw or make a mistake during a presentation, it is extremely unlikely you will die. But your body doesn't necessarily always see it that way.

Anxiety is the residue of that alarm system doing its job. We've evolved that way because the penalty of ignoring a physical threat to our safety is very severe. So we're wired with a "negative bias"—we pay way more attention to what could go wrong and hurt us than what is safe. That can make managing your emotions in a competitive situation far more challenging.

It means you need to learn how to channel anxiety and keep it in realistic proportion to the actual threat. Luckily that's something you can learn to do. Learning to relax is a skill that will help you improve your performance in many areas in your life. As Bill Murray once said on the topic, "The more relaxed you are, the better you are at everything: the better you are with your loved ones, the better you are with your enemies, the better you are at your job, the better you are with yourself."

Understanding Anxiety

Most people think of anxiety as something that happens automatically in response to a scary or stressful event or in anticipation of something bad happening—what's called "future-oriented worry." That might be true in the narrowest sense, but what feels like anxiety to you is actually an emotional response to the actual physical manifestations of biological arousal. When your body senses a potential threat it goes into what is called *physiological arousal*. How you respond physically, mentally, and emotionally to that condition of physiological arousal determines how "anxious" you ultimately feel.

It's certainly true that if you get hit with the signs of physiological arousal—rapid breathing, increased heart rate, muscle tension—and "let go of the wheel" mentally and emotionally and just give in to those sensations, you'll essentially be at the mercy of your instincts. That's a good way to stay alive, but it certainly isn't always the best way to hit a fastball in the ninth inning or ace an interview. Below I have listed a number of things that elite performers I have worked with worry about in their professional and everyday lives.

Ten Common Causes of Future-Oriented Worry

- Moving to a more competitive environment
- Competing for higher stakes
- Potential health concerns
- Job uncertainty
- Relationship stress with a partner, friend, or children
- Public speaking
- Financial uncertainty
- Unfamiliar social situations
- Dating
- Large-scale financial transactions (e.g., buying a home, buying a car)

Elite performers in sports and business haven't come up with a secret way to *eliminate* anxiety surrounding these situations; they just know how to recognize the level of anxiety they're feeling in the moment and then manage the physical effects of it. And "manage" is an important distinction too. The goal isn't to create a scenario where you have no emotional response to what is happening around you; the goal is to interpret your own level of arousal and then operate at the peak level of activation— enough arousal to be activated and sharp but not so much that you're out of control. In this chapter I'll show you some strategies for doing just that.

When you can confront anxiety or fear at the source by changing the way you think about something—by reframing the narrative—you can cut off some of those responses right away. We discuss that in the chapter on self-talk (Chapter 6) in that some worries can be dispelled by thinking about them differently. But there will be plenty of times when you face anxiety or fear that can't be controlled with self-talk. In other words, you're going to need an active strategy to manage that stress or anxiety. By training to prepare yourself for the stressful moments that come, you are able to show up with your best version of yourself wherever you are. In those cases it's important to start actively intervening in the process your body naturally wants to default to in its response to anxiety.

Commander Eric Potterat, head psychologist to the US Navy Seals and high performance consultant, is a leading expert on optimizing performance in extremely stressful environments. Eric gave me his perspective on how critical it is to train to be prepared for stress, "Whether it's the battlefield, the boardroom, the classroom, or the sport field, a successful performance starts and ends with mental performance. Those individuals who take the time to learn and practice well-researched and established mental adversity tolerance techniques are the individuals or teams that will more consistently perform optimally under pressure. The beauty here is that these techniques naturally transfer to other aspects of a person's life. Whatever job you have, from business to parenting, you will experience stress. The mental techniques that an athlete, a firefighter, a law enforcement officer, or a military member may use to navigate through a pressured situation 'on the job' will be the same ones that lead to adversity tolerance or stress resilience at home, with family and really with life in general. The techniques and curricula that I teach not only contribute to better performance, but they lead to better whole people."

When elite military units like the Navy SEALs go through training, they do plenty of physical work to get in peak condition. They also spend a tremendous amount of time on the mental and psychological components necessary for that very demanding job. In training, instructors drop the prospective SEALs into extremely stressful situations to both evaluate their natural responses to, say, being dropped in the ocean a mile from shore in full gear and to train them to respond to anxiety in a more controlled way.

One of the cornerstone techniques the SEALs—and plenty of world-class athletes and other performers—use is breathing training. In general terms you can take some control over your body's autonomous response to anxiety and stress by practicing certain breathing exercises. A well-established body of research says that the average person can significantly reduce the anxiety response by taking six full breaths—inhaling and exhaling—per minute.[1] In one study people experienced less anxiety and developed greater confidence after applying breathing techniques in therapy.[2] The act of both timing your breathing and practicing within the guidelines gives you more *physical* control of your body.

Few people know about managing stressful situations like Jason Brezler. Jason is a FDNY rescue fireman assigned to a special operations company in Brooklyn, New York. A major in the Marine Corp Reserve, Jason has served four combat tours in places that include Fallujah, Iraq, and Afghanistan. I've had the pleasure of collaborating with him and his group, Leadership Under Fire, a company that endeavors to enhance performance in firefighters and other high-risk professions with greater attention to mental-skills training.

One day, while we were working together on a training, he clarified the importance of anxiety management for elite firefighters. "When responding to a fire there are only a few minutes from the time of the alarm in the firehouse to the time when the fire trucks arrive at the fire," he said. "I have personally found it beneficial to work through a few breathing cycles while mentally rehearsing likely actions and visualizing the scenario. I think the value in breathing comes in controlling my heart rate. All of the science suggests that the ability to perform tactical tasks, whether they be searching, forcing a door, working off of a ladder, or even accurately communicating important info to others, are all contingent on arousal control and heart rate. The physical and mental demands involved when operating in an uncertain and dangerous environment naturally push a firefighter to a level of arousal that can be counterproductive to their mission. When you enter a smoke-filled home with limited to zero visibility it's imperative you enter with a plan. It's inevitable that your heart rate and respiratory rate are elevated. This is due to both the physical demands and the anxiety of operating in an environment where there is uncertainty. Additionally some senses that we as humans are heavily reliant on, like vision, are frequently diminished. Without mental skills like managing stress through breathing, it is easy to get overwhelmed. Without a strong mental foundation, your fitness and your tactical and technical acumen or skill set is going to be of much less value. You're going to have to maintain that state of mental fitness in order to apply your physical skills to prevent a negative outcome."

It's all a matter of scale. Although the negative outcomes that may arise if Jason isn't prepared to manage his anxiety are a matter of life and death, the same principles apply to an athletic event, meeting, presentation, or other important moment. The better you are at regulating your mental state and balancing anxiety, the more success and enjoyment you will derive from the situation.

Another way to effectively transform your feelings around being anxious is to change the way you evaluate the sensations you are experiencing. Essentially you're changing the "camera" with which you see the situation to a different angle.

Peak performers in sports, entertainment, and business are often able to take a detached, "third person" view of what they do. They're essentially watching themselves perform as if seeing it on video. When they "see" themselves experience discomfort, they watch more as an interested observer, not the person actually experiencing those feelings. Operating that way creates a kind of nonjudgmental awareness of their mental state—the ideal platform for channeling those moods and feelings in a productive way. When you can be willing to experience the feeling and sensations regarding your anxiety as normal and not harmful, you can gain a sense of power over them even though they haven't gone away.

By objectively examining your sensations and feelings in those situations and increasing your awareness and acceptance of those feelings as natural and "part of the deal," you're doing a lot of the work of deescalating the anxiety creating those feelings in the first place. In other words, telling yourself that the feelings of anxiety are normal, caused by your sympathetic nervous system, and actually helpful can reduce your discomfort when you're anxious and allow you to perform better with these feelings.

How do you actually do this? Practice a ritual in which you ask yourself three questions:

What is it that I am physically experiencing?

How do the sensations I'm experiencing begin and end?

How am I doing at having a positive interpretation about my experience?

Much of the discomfort that comes from anxiety or worry has to do with our contextualizing experiences as bad or good—and ourselves as bad or good for having them rather than simply telling ourselves that a particular sensation can't hurt us and is just what it is. It's natural as a human being to experience a wide variety of physical and mental experiences. In other words, it's not the objective stress that makes us truly uncomfortable but our evaluation or interpretation of that stressor.

Here's an example of that process in action.

It's the first week of the baseball season, and a rookie out-fielder comes up to bat for the first time in a home game. It's a big crowd, and they're all excited to see the new phenom that's been talked about all spring.

The rookie is certainly nervous when he comes to the plate the first time, and he takes a cut at the first pitch he sees and dribbles a weak roller to second base for an easy out. It doesn't get much better the second and third times up, as he strikes out and pops out to third base.

The fourth time up, there are two outs and a runner on third base. The rookie's team is down by a run, and coming through with a base hit would be a big deal. The opposing manager walks out slowly to talk to the pitcher—probably to remind him not to give in and to make the rookie swing the bat.

The rookie takes a step off the batter's box to collect his thoughts. He's in a new place, with a new team, but the scenario isn't new. He's had to come up to bat in big situations hundreds of times in his career. At first he feels his heart beating so hard, he can almost hear it in his ear. His breath is a bit too fast and shallow, and he feels as though he's playing in the tropics, even though it's a cool Midwestern spring afternoon. He talks to himself: "I'm just feeling some nerves right now. That's cool. It's just me getting ready to battle. This is what I've always dreamed of, getting a chance to swing the bat in the big leagues. How cool would it be to stroke one right here?" He then notes that he is breathing at a slightly rapid pace. He works to slow that down, counting to four with each inhalation and another four-second count for each exhalation, then taking a one- or two-second pause.

After taking a first-pitch strike, the rookie smiles to himself and knows he let one good opportunity go by: "Throw me another one—I'll be taking my best shot."

After two wasted pitches the pitcher throws a great off-speed pitch that almost fools the rookie. He's ahead of it but gets enough of the ball to hit a grounder through the gap. Knowing that mastering his physical sensations allowed him to perform at his best, he hands his batting gloves to the first-base coach and tells himself he can't wait to get in the situation again and have another chance to be the hero.

It's important to mention again that in the rookie's—or anybody else's—case, stepping up in a completely relaxed state wouldn't have been good at all. One of the most enduring and empirically supported laws in the history of psychology, the Yerkes-Dodson law, shows us that when people have too much physiological alarm they fail to perform well.[3] However, if they are too relaxed, in that they are not "amped" enough, their performance falters just as much.

What you're looking for is that ideal mix of situational awareness and energy but with *composure*—calmness and self-control. It will come as no surprise to learn that operating from a place of composure allows you to evaluate adversity and unexpected situations more accurately and seemingly in slow motion, whereas operating with a lack of composure often produces unfocused, panicked thought. It seems like events surrounding you are "out of control" or happening too quickly for you to handle. That negative sensation is so common for rookies in professional sports that the phrase "the game slowed down for me" has entered the common lexicon. In fact, the greatest players have a reputation for being able to "slow the game down." Reggie Jackson, the Hall of Fame baseball player, had this to say about another Yankees legend, Derek Jeter: "In big games, the action slows down for him, when it speeds up for others."[4] Jeter may be unique in his innate ability to perform in the clutch, but everyone can train to be ready to embrace the sensations of anxiety with a more effective approach. Once a player has gained training, experience, and composure, the events on the field "slow down" in the figurative sense and he or she feels integrated with the action as opposed to overwhelmed by it.

In my practice I see dozens of world-class athletes and performers with similar issues related to maintaining composure and managing anxiety—and what they're experiencing is the same thing any "normal" person would when placed under stress. The arenas might be different—say, a stadium filled with forty-five thousand people vs. a conference room at your work—but the emotional wiring is similar.

For anybody, from a Cy Young Award–winning pitcher to a salesperson, establishing a routine to address anxiety realistically and consistently lets you take much more control over your emotional and physical response in those situations. The right kind of routine helps you plow through some of the most common anxiety roadblocks we all face, like the expectation of perfection or the overwhelming need for approval.

You can let physiological and emotional responses to fear and pressure interfere with your ability to stay focused on the task at hand. You might feel yourself shaking or breathing erratically. Your mind might start to flood with negative "what if" thoughts, and you could start forecasting what it would mean to win or lose and the consequences of either.

That is completely normal.

What you do next spells the difference between giving in to the anxiety and breaking the cycle.

Part of that process comes from the breathing and self-talk exercises we've been talking about. Another part of it comes from the basic concept of mind-set. Dr. Carol Dweck's groundbreaking research revealed that people who have a "fixed" mind-set—the belief that their abilities were pretty much static and inborn and couldn't be changed—did not perform as well as people with a "growth" mind-set, defined as the belief that abilities can be shaped and improved.[5]

I think we can all agree that, in theory, having a growth mind-set is far more preferable than having a fixed one. But what does that look like in practice? And how does that relate to managing your biological alarm or anxiety level?

Go back to the example of the rookie hitter from earlier in the chapter. If he operated with a fixed mind-set, he would be thinking to himself during that first week of the season that he made the big leagues based on his natural talent, that his eyes and his reflexes were going to help him hit those fastballs. That's fine, but what happens the first time he goes into a slump? How will he react when he feels all the natural physical reactions of his body preparing for his debut? Because of the fixed mind-set and a belief that talents are innate and not developed, a period of struggle will have him questioning those "innate" talents and doubting himself. If you're constantly asking yourself whether you're really good enough to be there, it's hard to actually *be* there.

However, operating from a growth mind-set allows the player to both embrace his natural talents—which, of course, he has lots—and *learn* from negative experiences. Going through pressure experiences by themselves doesn't make it easier to handle pressure; it's learning what do to and applying those anxiety-management techniques the next time. If the player strikes out on a particularly nasty pitch, he's adding that to the memory banks and reducing his chance of getting fooled next time. He's also able to operate from a much more positive mind-set: "I didn't get a hit this time, but I'm learning from it and doing the things I need to do to get a hit next time."

There is an opportunity here for you as well. Any unwanted result (the O of DOT) is an opportunity for you to question your ability or look for what you can do to improve or grow. In addition, this idea has a direct impact on your ability to respond in an adaptive way to situations that make you anxious. When you sense yourself getting anxious about a presentation, meeting, or other important event, work to message yourself in a way that puts the physiological sensations in perspective. For example, let's say you are about to stand up and give a presentation to your colleagues and, like our rookie, feel your heart racing. In that situation it's more productive to say, "This is just my body getting me ready" than "Oh no! I'm about to lose it, where's the exit?" Moreover, taking the growth mind-set approach and saying, "This is an opportunity to try out my *Life as Sport* techniques" rather than solely focusing on the outcome will help you to stay committed to improving, no matter what the result.

Physical Approaches to Managing Anxiety

Improving mind-set isn't magic. It just takes awareness, conscious work, and maybe even a little acting. We're all wired to interpret nonverbal communication to determine whether someone else is angry, romantically interested, in pain, happy, angry, and so on. We then take this information and make decisions on how we will proceed in our interactions with that individual. A player who walks with "swagger" communicates to his opponents, teammates, coaches, and himself that he expects to do well and, if given the opportunity, he will. A player who acts overtly discouraged, fearful, or agitated communicates to his opponents, coaches, and teammates that he is easily defeated or unfocused. This behavior can fuel an opponent's resolve or damage your team's confidence in you. More importantly this behavior may communicate defeat to the one person who needs you most: yourself. The way in which we behave sends messages to our body about how we feel.

Many years ago I worked with a pitcher who was having trouble with his command. A big tall right-hander with a crushing fastball, he was having trouble locating the ball and was also hitting a lot of batters. These negative outcomes were coupled with the fact that he had what he called "bad" defense behind him, which led to very poor body language when he walked a batter or allowed a hit. If an opposing player got a hit—especially if it was a hit that the pitcher felt a fielder could have prevented—he would punch his glove as though he was attacking the infielder who had missed the play. He would then shake his head as though lamenting having to go into bankruptcy. He would hang his head and kick the dirt on the mound.

I'm not saying those emotional responses were wrong; there's no doubt sports—or any other competitive endeavor—can be frustrating. But how you allow those frustrations to physically manifest themselves goes a long way toward how you actually process those frustrations. Your body reacts to what your mind does, but your mind also reacts to your body.

Consider this fascinating study, undertaken by Drs. Fritz Strack, Leonard Martin, and Sabine Stepper in 1988. Using three groups of people, they asked each group to hold a pen a different way—in their lips, teeth, or nondominant hand. The group holding the pen in their teeth was basically being forced to smile, while the group holding it in their lips was being forced to frown. The group holding it in their nondominant hand was the control. The doctors discovered that the group holding the pen in their teeth—so that the muscles in their face were "forced" into a smile—objectively found a certain cartoon significantly funnier than the other two groups. In other words, the physical act of smiling influenced the emotion of happiness or enjoyment.[6]

Now think to yourself what a winning player looks like. Imagine a star baseball player when he hits a walk-off home run as his teammates rush onto the field. Or the reaction of a gold medalist as she realizes she has won the hundred-meter dash. What are the physical actions they display upon this exciting victory?

With rare exceptions, they do the same thing. They raise their arms over their heads in fists in a "V" for victory formation. It doesn't matter where they are from or what language they speak; it is the human reaction to being victorious.

Put this book down and try it yourself. Stand up, raise your arms over your head, make fists with your hands, and pump your arms in the air as though you just won a heavyweight fight. If you feel like extra credit, jump up and down a bit. Let out a shout: "Yeahhhhhh!"

Feels good, right? We'll get back to that. Now try the opposite. Mimic the actions of a person who has just lost. Drop your head and sulk. Really get dejected. How did that feel?

Getting back to our pitcher and his glove-punching display, I asked him what he thought happened when the other team saw him react that way. "The next guy up probably can't wait to get his chance," he said. It also didn't help his relationship with his teammates any. They didn't love getting shown up after every mistake.

Sure, opponents and teammates feed both negatively and positively off your emotional reactions. But the most powerful outcome of negative composure and body language is the effect it has on *your* feelings and self-confidence. If you sulk and bow your head, you are telling your body how to feel. You are saying, "I am a loser" with your body and posture more clearly than if you yelled it at the top of your lungs. Your body and mind will cooperate, and you'll start to feel far less capable and confident.

The pitcher in this story became very motivated to change his composure. We developed a system to work on more positive body posture and composure. In sports as in life, it's always easier to concentrate on doing something vs. not doing something. Instead of focusing on not slumping his shoulders, I asked him imagine he had a string coming out of the middle of his chest right between his pectoral muscles, like a puppet. When something went wrong, he would imagine pulling this string so his shoulders would widen. He also picked a focal point above his eye line, a flag in the distance, and make sure he looked up at it instead of down in the dirt. These two small physical adjustments kept him from contorting his body into postures that would leave him feeling less confident and, thus, less ready to throw the next pitch. The simple physical adjustments sent messages back to his body that helped to repurpose his physiological arousal and what he might call "stress" or "frustration." Additionally, when he was practicing this form of stress management, it allowed him to focus on something neutral, and the result was that his mind was not obsessing over the negative outcome.

I watched him every outing and would give him feedback on how much he was able to keep his composure and adapt to a more confident, ready body position. You can do the same for your performances in living life as sport. Once you practice the exercises below, you will master the fine-tuned instrument of your body and be able to defeat the lions inside and out.

How-To: Breathing Training:
The Key to Controlling Anxiety

Learning how to slow one's body down is the most important thing for being able to perform at your best and overcome anxiety. We know that some degree of physiological arousal is necessary for peak performance but that too much arousal (anxiety) can negatively affect ability. A reliable way to induce the relaxation response is through regulating your breathing. Regulating breathing has many benefits. First, it slows down biological alarm or sympathetic nervous system (flight or fight) activity and helps your parasympathetic nervous system kick in and help you calm down. Second, it aids in the process of managing stress so you can make calm decisions and react in the best way possible. Finally, breathing regulation can be a part of a powerful routine to get your mind and body in the most adaptive state in order to perform at your best.

Breathing training is simple and can be practiced for as little as five minutes a day. It is ideal to take approximately six full breaths per minute. Although it is nearly impossible to time six breaths perfectly, this goal can be achieved by counting the number of seconds of each inhalation and exhalation. Begin by trying to regulate your breath into nine- to ten-second cycles: four seconds for each inhalation and four seconds for each exhalation followed by a one- to two-second pause. While breathing in, in your mind count, "one-one-thousand, two-one-thousand, three-one-thousand, four-one-thousand." On exhalation do the same thing, counting, "one-one-thousand, two-one-thousand, three-one-thousand, four-one-thousand." Then pause for one or two seconds and start the process all over again. Try to focus on bringing breaths in by inflating your diaphragm, the muscle right below your rib cage, and pushing your breath out by deflating or sucking in your abdomen, pressing down with your diaphragm. Imagine there is a balloon in your stomach that inflates when you bring the breath in with each inhalation and deflates with each exhalation. If this is challenging, it is fine to just focus on timing your breaths and leave off the diaphragmatic breathing component.

You could argue that almost nobody on earth knows more about breathing than Laird Hamilton. A legendary big-wave surfer, Hamilton pioneered the sport of tow-in surfing—finding the world's largest waves out in the middle of the ocean and getting towed in to ride them in literally a death-defying way. He needs to understand how to breathe to not only reduce anxiety but also stay alive after getting crushed by a giant wave. He once described to me how important breathing exercises are to him. "They let you actually go into a deep meditative state almost instantaneously and almost mechanically," Laird said. "The fact is, before there were instruments that could keep us alive, our spirit was directly connected to our breath. Meditation is a way to become intimate with your spirit, which is ultimately with yourself. It's all connected to your breath."

To further increase your relaxation you can practice self-talk or a mantra in your mind between breaths: statements such as, "I am more relaxed now than I was before that breath" or "I am ready for this challenge because _____." Practicing this breathing for five minutes each day will help you be more resilient to stress. There is even some evidence that this type of breathing and other mindfulness training is so powerful, it has helped Navy SEALs avoid PTSD.[7] The more we practice this breath work, the more useful it will be in moments of actual stress during performance. As this type of breathing becomes more natural to you, it will be more reflexive to use it to relax your body for peak performance in competition. Breathing in this way can also be used as a stress-management technique or as part of visualization (imagery) training.

How-To: Composure Experiment and Practice

Either record or have someone observe your performance, presentation, or meeting, and note one or two things you could do behaviorally (the D of DOT) to improve your demonstration of confidence, strength, or self-assuredness. Design a few behaviors to improve your composure. Here are some things you could work on improving:

- Your posture: How much do you slouch or stand with your chest held high?
- The position of your gaze: Are you keeping your eyes at the level of your audience?
- Eye contact: How much are you making? Experiment with the balance.
- Smiling: Practice smiling while listening and speaking.
- Uncrossing your arms/legs: Work on having an "open" posture.

The more you work on purposefully practicing these composure exercises, the more relaxed and less anxious you are likely to feel.

Enjoyment Exercise

As humans we are naturally programmed to notice what's wrong. One way to enjoy your experience more is to work to notice what is going right. Try to take time out of the day to notice, appreciate, and enjoy moments in which you are not feeling anxious or stressed. You might set an hourly reminder on your phone that prompts you to check in with yourself. Noting all the times that we are not feeling uncomfortable or anxious can help put into perspective the times when we are. And while you're at it, feel free to appreciate anything else that's going well with your body and mind. For example, you might say to yourself or a friend, "Right now I am grateful my body feels relaxed" or "I'm noticing that I am alert and ready to perform right now."

5

Visualization

Unlock the Power of Your Mind

If you think spring training is the time major league baseball players come in and *start* to get ready for the upcoming season, you seriously underestimate how much work goes into being one of the few hundred best players on the planet.

When I first started working with professional baseball players I had a conversation with a now all-star player. I remember it as if it happened yesterday. We were talking about all of the physical work he had been doing over the course of the offseason to come into spring training in peak condition, and he mentioned how much *mental* work he put in during that same stretch.

"By the time I get to spring training I've already had thousands of at-bats in my mind," he told me. "That's an advantage."

It shouldn't be a surprise, then, that multiple studies show that athletes who reach the top levels of professional and Olympic sports are far more likely to use mental visualization—the strategy of picturing yourself successfully accomplishing a task—than those who don't use visualization.[1]

It's appropriate to talk about visualization within the context of the physical workouts the player was also doing because just like lifting weights or practicing hitting in the cage, visualization is something that can be learned, practiced, and improved.

In this chapter I'll show you how to do it.

Let's start with a simple exercise.

Imagine I've handed you a perfectly cut lemon wedge. Take the wedge in your hand and picture slowly bringing it up to your mouth. Bite into the juicy, bitter pulp. Now close your eyes and do it again—this time bringing your hand toward your mouth as though you have a real piece of lemon in your fingers.

What kind of sensations did you experience when you did this? I bet some of you actually got the sense of bitterness in your mouth or swallowed reflexively a few times.

Inside the human mind thoughts and imagery have tremendous power. They can—and do—influence physical performance and emotional well-being to a huge degree. An elite athlete can train his or her body to the absolute apex of physical condition, but if he or she doesn't train the mind, that physical effort can be wasted. A poorly tuned mind gets in the way of the great physical tools and talents that could produce great success.

It happens all the time, both on playing fields and in other walks of life. I've had professional musicians come to me and describe a typical situation. They go through a brutal practice schedule of five or six hours per day to master technique, only to find that they perform poorly in concert because they have low self-confidence or performance anxiety when they get to the stage. Many of my clients from the financial sector used to struggle with the relentlessness of the markets and the grind that comes with staying on top of the information flood. They learned to spend fifteen to twenty minutes a day practicing the visualization techniques specific to their business, which works as a kind of pressure relief valve, and many of them scored landmark results.

You can use the same tools to make the most of your practice time, whether your aim is to excel in hitting a ball, playing a cello, making a stock trade, leading a meeting, or teaching your kid a new concept. They are all living life as sport, and visualization will be a powerful key to unlock your talents.

Experience It Before You Do It

Visualization is a powerful tool because it helps your mind prepare your body for what's coming. While researchers are still seeking out the exact reason why visualization works, there's no doubt that visualization triggers parts of our neuromuscular system. As far back as the 1930s, researchers such as Edmund Jacobson found that visualization triggered low-level electrical activity in the muscles that are much less intense than if the activity has been actually performed. More contemporary researchers have studied EMG activity in the muscles with different kinds of visualizations. One of the questions being asked currently in this research is the specificity of muscles that are triggered when imagining a task, which has much larger implications why and how visualization improves performance. Research seems to go both ways on this question. The bottom line is that when you visualize, your body has a physical reaction and the act of visualization has been associated with performance gains.[2]

That's just as true for an Olympic sprinter or award-winning actor as it is for a commodities trader. "Before I go to an event or a meeting, I'll prepare for that experience as if it were a show," says actor and *Entourage* star Adrian Grenier. "What kind of performance do I want to give here? Who do I want to be?

What is the outcome? And then I go through the mental process of creating that outcome in my mind. A lot of times people
want the outcome without participating in the necessary steps
to get there. It's as if the actor goes up on the stage to perform—
without a script, without a costume, without having done the
work to embody the character. They just stand there silent, in-
ept. Unless you practice the traits of the character and become
them, you won't be that person, at least not when the curtain
opens and it's showtime." As Adrian demonstrated, visualization
is part of how you transfer a goal from an internal place—your
head—to an external place like the stage . . . or your life.

In other words, you're getting essentially the same "experience" benefit by vividly picturing yourself doing something
ahead of time as you would by actually doing it. Of course, that
doesn't mean you can picture Serena Williams's serve for a week
and then go play in your club match with a new 120-miles-per-
hour weapon. But by visualizing *your own* serve and the things
you need to do with it in order to hit it well, you're getting virtually the same benefit you would as if you went to the club and
hit two hundred practice serves.

At the elite level in sports, visualization serves another, even
more important purpose of helping the athlete compete without anxiety. By visualizing every step of the process, a professional golfer knows exactly what will happen from the moment
he decides what shot to hit to when he's done swinging the club
and beginning to walk to the next shot. And by mentally practicing each scenario multiple times, you're preparing yourself for
the stress involved in the performance situation and have far less
of a chance of being surprised by your emotional response.
You've essentially "inoculated" yourself to pressure. If you have
faced a particular opponent in your head, it is less stressful to
face it in the real world.

How does it work?

There are a series of theories scientists have established to try to explain the neurological underpinnings of visualization. Like a lot of brain research, we don't have all the answers yet, but it seems to hinge on a few key areas. One theory holds that visualizing an event causes the brain to actually fire the muscles needed to produce the motion in a small way, building a neuromuscular pattern that can be accessed later.[3]

Another theory says that imagery gives the mind a subconscious plan for a series of complicated activities, and the plan then works as a road map when it's actually time to perform the activities. A third theory says that visualization offers a kind of psychological exercise, a way of building mental muscles that give a person increased concentration and confidence and protection against anxiety.[4]

It doesn't matter which of those theories is the most accurate or if it's more of a combination of all of them—the proof is in the results. With a simple, step-by-step process you can develop the same visualization skills that elite athletes and businesspeople use to compete and set records at the highest level of achievement. Not only can anybody learn the techniques, but the skills themselves are transferrable to any physical or mental process you want to improve.

Going up to bat with two outs in the bottom of the ninth and the bases loaded in a tied game is, in many ways, like taking a final exam, making a job-saving business pitch, executing a series of essential financial trades, or having a crucial conversation with a family member. Visualizing it beforehand gives you the opportunity to enter these situations with the confidence of someone who has already succeeded.

Before you start thinking to yourself that this is some kind of foreign language you have to learn, visualization, or guided imagery, is something you're probably already doing on one level or another every day. If you're somebody who makes out a schedule for your day and perhaps thinks about the conversations you're going to have, you're visualizing. When you plot out a route in your mind that you're going to drive, seeing the landmarks along the way, you're visualizing.

The only difference between those examples and what elite athletes and business people do when they practice dedicated visualization is that they're doing it in full color, using all the powers of our very powerful brains. They—and soon you—are fine tuning their imagery and changing all the components to make sure their brain is practicing in the way that has been shown to help people succeed.

Take Sam Kass, for example, the former White House chef and nutrition adviser. Sam has found that visualization has been very effective for him in both cooking and policy making. "Visualization was always really important and I definitely use it a lot," he told me. "Seeing what is going to happen and playing it out and practicing it in my mind seems to be almost bizarrely powerful. You can almost will the outcome you were hoping for by seeing it. I have used visualization to have a clear vision on what I want to do in the kitchen or in dealing with policy planning. Being able to close your eyes and think about yourself performing as you would like to helped me while working at the White House, and it will help you to not get blown off course by all the various forces that are influencing the outcome in your life. Cooking is straightforward. You need to learn how to envision a dish. I remember when I was first starting, one of the first guys who helped train me told me, 'You have to learn how to taste in your mind.' I was like, huh? He continued, 'You'll be able to taste in your mind and imagine how things taste and put together a dish in your head. When you do, the dish will be better when you actually make it.' When he first said that, it sounded strange. But quickly it became pretty clear about how effective visualization was when I practiced it. So whether it's making a new dish or developing an elaborate strategy for expanding food access to low-income families, I'll always envision what I'm planning to do in detail in my mind before I do it. What would a policy announcement look like in order to have a big impact? The more I visualize it and practice in my mind, the more objective success I'm likely to have."

One of my main goals in this chapter—and in this book—is to demystify some of the processes elite performers use to improve their results. Sure, some people are initially naturally better at visualizing than others. Everybody is wired differently. But there are plenty of athletes, business people, and others who weren't so good at visualizing but practiced and got to be very good.

The basic visualization "skill" is the ability to mentally rehearse a scenario. In the context of sports, an athlete will use the powers of imagination to close his eyes and pretend to step into a scenario and imagine in detail what it feels like to perform in a certain way and how he or she responds to the mental, physical, and emotional cues during the scenario. All of the senses are incorporated, so a baseball player getting ready to hit would be seeing the pitcher in front of him, just like in real life. He'd hear the roar of the crowd and feel the smooth wood of the bat in his hands and the stickiness of the pine tar on the handle.

As this mental rehearsal skill gets enhanced, a player can continually replay the visualization on a loop and see hundreds or thousands of at-bats. The player is actually training his mind and body to perform in the way he sees the events unfolding in his mind. When done properly, it's a hugely effective tool for building confidence and self-belief.

Going back to the all-star baseball player we talked about at the beginning of the chapter, his hitting visualization was extremely vivid, specific—and even varied. When he pictured those hundreds of pitches coming his way, he saw everything, from the way the pitcher lifted his lead leg to the way his hand appeared when he released the ball. He saw a variety of different pitches (and pitchers)—fastballs, breaking balls, sliders, and even pitches in the dirt. In some visualizations he pictured himself making square, hard contact. He pictured himself rounding the bases and getting the pats on the helmet from his teammates. In others he pictured himself taking bad pitches and being selective. And in others he even pictured himself getting fooled on a pitch and swinging and missing—so he could prepare himself for reacting adaptively to the emotions that came with that.

Starting with the basics, the best way to visualize is to see it as if you're watching it from your own eyes, in what is called the "associated" view. A "disassociated" view happens when you visualize as if you're watching yourself perform in a movie or a highlight film. Watching from the associated view tends to give you more connection to the feelings and emotions that come with the visualized scenario; but doing it in a disassociated way is better than not doing it at all.

Actually choosing what you visualize is more than just picking yourself doing something great and winning all the prizes. Because your mind can't differentiate between practice that's happening in real life and practice that's happening in your mind, it *is* important to visualize constructive, specific things. But if you simply visualize outcomes—like holding up the trophy at the end of the day—you aren't seeing the actual performance pieces that make your physical motions more efficient and effective. It doesn't mean that kind of visualization is worthless; it just means you aren't getting as much out of the technique as you could.

Think about why you practice anything—a presentation, the piano, any sports movement. The repetition of that activity ingrains in the mind and body the way you want your mind and body to perform when it matters in response to a certain situation. Effective visualization replicates that concept but leaves out the physical part. It's a blueprint that gives the brain a picture of the best version of yourself—and it gives the body a chance to re-create that image in real time. The more clear, concise, and applicable the information you provide in the form of that blueprint, the more quickly and efficiently your brain can interpret that information and relay it to your body for peak performance.

This process is no different from the one you already employ—subconsciously—when you perform a deceivingly complicated task like walking. Walking is something we all learn to do when we're very small, and it's something most of us have never consciously thought much about. But if you broke down all the muscle movements, balance, and coordination that has to happen for you to successfully walk, it would probably consume all of your frontline brain power. The same is true for any activity that becomes "second nature," like a golf swing for a PGA Tour player or a swing for a major league baseball player. Those players have created shortcuts in their minds to perform those physical tasks as second nature, like walking.

Visualization is the skill that helps create those shortcuts.

Many of the baseball players I've worked with over the years have come from Latin America. Because I speak Spanish fluently, I have come to deeply understand the extreme amount of competition between kids in many countries to be recognized by major league scouts and get the chance to enter the feeder system that eventually spits the best player out into the big leagues.

Because there are so many players clamoring for the limited attention of a relatively small number of scouts, the players have come up with a simple saying about making the most of your opportunity: As I have heard said in the Dominican Republic, for example, "You don't *walk* off the island." That means that the skill of being selective about the quality of pitch you swing at—a skill highly valued by major league teams—is short-circuited at the introductory level by players who (understandably) want to show scouts how they can swing the bat.

But what often happens when the small handful of players who catch a scout's eye actually make it into the minor leagues and want to work their way up to the big club? All of a sudden they're being asked to identify pitcher tendencies and avoid swinging at bad pitches—skills that have usually gone completely against every ounce of instinct and training those players have received their whole career.

When faced with those requirements, what can a player who has been trained to be non-selectively aggressive do? If he waits to see the thousands of pitches he needs to build that pitch-recognition skill, he won't make it to the majors until his late twenties—too late for a prospect. If he never learns to be selective at the plate, he might not *ever* make it to the majors.

But if that player learns to visualize, he can make thousands of swings at anything he wants in his mind and get virtually the same benefit as he would if he stood in the box and took all those pitches for real. He can supercharge the improvement process and come up and be a factor on the big team months or years before he might have otherwise. That could easily be a $25 million difference in career earnings.

I'd say that potential makes it worth it to spend a few minutes learning how best to enter the visualizing state. Ideally you want to find a quiet place where you can visualize in a relaxed state of mind. When you can silence the natural chatter in your mind, you're giving yourself a much better chance of receiving the message. For some of my baseball clients this means finding a quiet spot in the clubhouse a few hours before the game to zone out with some headphones on, visualizing pitches coming out of that night's opposing pitcher's hand and stroking them successfully into the gaps. The surfer Laird Hamilton has the benefit of spending most of his "work" time in a natural environment without a lot of distractions. "There's something about nature that kind of allows the brain to turn off and the visualization side to turn on," Hamilton told me. "I think being in places that allow your brain to be free and unencumbered—being open to those channels that allow you to see the things you want to see and visualize the things you want to happen. One thing about the ocean—the act of riding a wave itself is a form of meditation."

You might not have access to the Pacific Ocean as easily as Laird does from Malibu or Kauai, but you can find your own quiet place. For somebody getting ready to go into a crucial sales call, it might be some zone-in time in the front seat of the car in the parking lot before walking into the building, picturing how the beginning of the presentation goes. Or a few minutes walking around outside in a park or other green area just to get some quiet and fresh air.

If you aren't using the visualization tool at all, any amount you try is going to have a positive benefit. But the more you do—and the more consistent you can be with it—the more you'll benefit from it.

The most talented practitioners in professional sports really *feel* what it's like for the ball to hit their hands or how the bases feel under their feet as they round them. They connect to the emotions that come with success, and they add as much detail into each visualization as possible. They often tell me that when they get to the biggest stage, like a playoff game, they're amazed at how similar the real experience is to what they pictured in their minds hundreds of times before. They "prelived" the moment, so they were much more ready for it when it actually happened.

Outcomes vs. Results

One of the most common visualization mistakes to make is to focus your mind on outcomes vs. results—in other words, focusing on the O of DOT rather than the D and T. Many top-level athletes I coach come to me with a visualization strategy they already use, but what they're doing isn't the most useful thing for elite performance: they aren't optimizing their visualization. Usually it means they're fantasizing about succeeding and being the hero instead of actually visualizing the process of getting the hit, completing a pass, or making a buzzer-beating shot.

In effective visualization you're putting up the scaffolding to support your practice. You're seeing all of the physical motions you've learned how to do, and you're seeing yourself perform them in a controlled, calm flow. You're setting up a system of markers that your body can follow the next time. Your mental practice centers around what you are *doing* with your muscles and what you are *thinking* with your self-talk.

It's important to stress again that visualization needs to be positive, but that doesn't mean that everything you visualize is the hero shot. You want to see yourself performing on the field—or giving the presentation from the podium—in a loose but realistic way. That means seeing yourself fly out or strike out from time to time as a baseball player or fielding a tough question from the crowd or having your PowerPoint presentation tech crap out on you as a businessperson. You want to see yourself performing well and handling adversity within those performances with calmness and good decision making. Seeing yourself handle less-than-ideal situations in your mind makes you far more prepared to handle them with a level head when they happen for real.

And they will.

Let's say you're that person giving the presentation. You probably want what everybody would want in that circumstance: an alert, attentive, appreciative crowd. When you visualize yourself giving that presentation, you need to be seeing yourself doing the things that would cause people to react that way. You could imagine your posture and your excellent eye contact, and you could vividly practice saying what you intend to say with vigor and focus. The more clearly you do this in your mental practice, the more visualization will help you integrate your skills so when it's time to talk for real, you'll take that calm sense of flow right to the podium.

Tennis pro Rennae Stubbs and her women's doubles partner had a string of close calls in major championships where they had missed opportunities to win the biggest titles for the first time. After those losses Rennae decided she was going to use visualization to reduce her anxiety about potentially "failing" in the big moment again. It was fascinating to hear her describe the process.

"A friend of mine with the same kind of personality—very hyper, very up and down—told me I should try picturing ahead of time what it would be like to be playing in the doubles final," Rennae told me excitedly. "So in the few days before, when I walked to the bathroom, I'd literally picture myself walking onto the court for that match, and I'd examine how that made me feel, in a kind of dress rehearsal for the real thing." I could just hear in her voice how much she enjoyed the process of using imagery to be her best.

Former NFL fullback Mike Robinson took a fascinating path to his professional career. As a college player at Penn State, Robinson was the Big Ten player of the year in 2005 as a quarterback but also played significant time at running back and wide receiver. Drafted into the NFL by the San Francisco 49ers, Robinson was converted from quarterback to running back and then took over the starting fullback job when the previous starter got hurt.

Many players would have struggled with changing roles, but Robinson—a three-time all–Big Ten academic award winner who earned two bachelor's degrees while at Penn State—embraced the challenge. "I visualized everything that could happen to me on every single play—every scenario, every coverage. The one thing I never wanted to be was surprised," Robinson told me. "You watch film and look at the game plan every week, but I would take that and play the game in my head ahead of time. Then you can call on the same thoughts and emotion during the real game because you've done it before and you've felt it before. You're bringing some calm to the chaos because you're ready and you've practiced it before in your mind. You have your plan, and now you're just following the directions."

How-To:
Step-by-Step Visualization Guide

If you went to see a physical trainer at the gym, he or she would give you a step-by-step exercise plan. You'd know that you needed to work five different exercises to strengthen your core on day one and then six different ones to build lower-body strength on day two, and so on.

Visualization is learnable in exactly the same way.

The following steps will give you a blow-by-blow account of how to train yourself in the skill of visualization. It doesn't matter if you've never pictured yourself doing a single thing in your life. If you follow the steps, your visualization "muscle" will get stronger.

Use it to map out any performance you want to improve—whether it's a sport, presentation, conversation, or even a first date—and your performance will improve, usually dramatically. Remember, though, that this is a kind of practice, and just like bench presses or bicep curls, it takes time for the "muscle" to go from disengaged to thriving.

The steps below are the exact ones I used to help many rookie league players to build on their physical talents and burst into the major leagues, where they now anchor the heart of the batting order.

1. Sit in a quiet place with your eyes closed.

2. Practice the Breathing Relaxation Exercise from Chapter 4.

3. Visualize yourself in the performance setting.

4. Make sure you use all of your senses to imagine the scene in which you will perform. (Seeing, touching, hearing, smelling, and tasting.)

5. Visualize your routine. (May be enhanced after reading chapter 7.)

6. See everything through your eyes in real time.

7. Get into your starting position to perform.

8. Make a positive self-statement or mantra (see Chapter 6).

9. Visualize your action in the most productive, efficient way possible.

10. Work on feeling your body doing well at executing the action you are trying to make.

11. Visualize varied results.

12. Experience overall positive but realistic results.

13. Imagine yourself reacting well with good self-talk and composure.

14. When you open your eyes try to notice what was *enjoyable* about this practice.

Enjoyment Exercise

Practice doing some imagery regarding an experience or situation unrelated to any goals you're working on. You can try this simply as a way to relax and enjoy the moment. For example, use the visualization technique that you've learned in this chapter to re-create a positive experience you've had on a vacation or with a friend or family member. Or create an imaginary scene of natural beauty (e.g., ocean, mountain, desert, forest) to help you enjoy a moment of peace wherever you happen to be.

6

Self-Talk

The Key to Confidence

You've heard it before—and have probably even *said* it before.

"Story of my life . . . "

It's the middle of a stretch of bad luck or bad outcomes, and one more unpleasant thing comes piling on. A flight gets canceled. An important client backs out of a meeting and takes his or her business to somebody else. A player is making the familiar walk from the shower to his locker the week before spring training ends and slips and breaks his leg.

"That's pretty much the story of my life," he says.

If you've said those words (or ones like them) to yourself, you might think they're a natural response to the frustration that comes from an unfortunate series of events. It *is* natural, but the words aren't just a response to negative events; they're actually reinforcing a pessimistic, negative perception you have about yourself and your future.

Say them often enough, and you'll actually start expecting negative things to happen in your life, a way of living that may contribute to blocking your path to success.

When I'm working with a client who says something like that in a session, I'll stop them with a simple question: "What *is* the story of your life?"

At first they're a little confused about what kind of answer I want. I explain to them that we all have a "life story" we tell ourselves in order to make sense of our experiences. If you're a salesperson with twenty years of record-breaking experience at your company and you get shut out by a client, you would probably react to that event internally and emotionally in a different way from how a beginner in his or her first week on the job would.

In the world of athletics somebody like Tom Brady has a different "life story" running through his head during a playoff football game than a younger, less experienced quarterback. That inner "soundtrack" lets him process things on the field much differently and recover more quickly from mistakes. "It could be a bad play that happened or an interception or a turnover or something, and [Brady] would come to the sideline and say, 'Okay, let's talk about what happened on that play,'" said New England Patriots head coach Bill Belichick. "He would say, 'This is what I saw. This is what happened. This is what this guy did, this is what that guy did, this is what the safeties did, this middle linebacker was here. This is what I saw on the route.' Then you go back and look at the film and all those things happened. The six, seven, eight, nine things that he described were pretty much the way the play unfolded."[1]

The actual in-the-moment narrative of that life story is called "self-talk," and it's something every person does almost constantly throughout every day. It's the stream-of-consciousness inner dialogue you have about yourself and all the things happening in your life. Your confidence—and your ability to perform at the peak of your abilities—is directly connected to the quality, frequency, and makeup of that self-talk. If you examine

Brady's self-talk, one critical element is missing: negative self-appraisal. He isn't berating himself; he is simply looking for ways to make himself better and having neutral or positive self-talk even when things go wrong. This allows him to mobilize in the face of adversity.

In simpler terms, improving your self-talk improves your self-confidence and self-esteem. And improved self-confidence and self-esteem are the cornerstones of improved mental performance. After all, nobody can be perfect all the time. As hitting legend Dave Winfield reminds me from time to time, "Slumps are to be thought of as 'periods of adjustment.' They are just 'statistically acceptable variations.'" Now that is some hall-of-fame self-talk!

In this chapter you're going to learn how elite athletes and business performers actually train their own self-talk—and create a better "life story"—in ways that boost confidence, optimism, and mental toughness.

It isn't about fooling yourself into believing something about yourself that isn't true; it's about *revealing* authentically positive and confidence-building storylines that exist but might not be at the front of your mind. For example, many of my baseball clients go through common growing pains during their first year in the big leagues. They might have some early success, but then the scouting reports go around, and the next circuit around the league gets to be tougher. When the slumps get deep enough, even the most naturally confident player can wonder whether he belongs. I'll ask the player some questions designed to remind him of the successes he had that got him where he is: "I hit .305 in Triple-A last year," or "I can throw my fastball wherever I want."

Working with those facts, the players can then work to re-establish a more positive, confident inner monologue.

It's something you can learn how to do too.

Much of the work in self-talk is derived from a style of therapy called *cognitive behavioral therapy*, which was initially developed to treat depression and anxiety.[2] This form of therapy is very similar to some aspects of sport psychology in that it takes an active directive and pragmatic approach to coaching people and developing strategies to deal with their problems. The renowned cognitive behavioral psychologist Dr. David Barlow developed a way of thinking about changing thoughts regarding anxiety that I use quite extensively in my work with athletes and performers. Dr. Barlow talks about two main errors in our thinking about ourselves that lead to a negative self-concept or feeling: *jumping to conclusions* and *blowing things out of proportion.*[3]

Before we introduce methods to help you to build adaptive responses to these two errors of thinking, let's examine what these maladaptive thought patterns are and how they work.

Jumping to Conclusions

When we jump to conclusions, we take a bit of information from the world and make a judgment about ourselves, others, or our environment. But "one swallow a summer does not make." In other words, if you see one lone bird traveling north, it's not safe to assume that the summer has arrived. The bird could be lost or an escaped pet, or perhaps it's a robot bird designed by an ingenious eighth grader. If we see the bird and take that one piece of information to mean that there has been a change of seasons, we are incorrectly using real information to guide our thinking down an erroneous path. Generalizations we make about ourselves and our performance based on incomplete or flawed information can be damaging to our self-esteem and, ultimately, our confidence.

Many years ago I was working with a very successful baseball pitcher when he was in the minor leagues a few games away from breaking into the "show." This pitcher was very astute about the principles of sport psychology. He had read all of the most popular performance psychology books and had even watched some online tutorials before we began to work together. This allowed us to operate at an extremely advanced pace and to use a comfortable psychology vocabulary in discussing ways we would work together on his actions and reactions. The pitcher was already dominating his competition, but he knew that working on his "mental conditioning" could help him excel even more than he already had. We worked together to develop a highly sophisticated mental practice routine that he practiced twice a day except on days when he was pitching—because he felt that this interfered with his ability to enter the game with a calm and focused mind.

One day I watched him pitch seven hitless innings. Even though we try not to focus on the results in performance psychology, it's still exhilarating to work with athletes of this caliber and see all of their mental practice pay off. In my mind I was cheering louder and louder with every strike he threw. Fans were hanging on the edges of their seats, the tension growing with each pitch. His pregame and in-game routines, which we will discuss in more detail in the next chapter, were working! A no-hitter was a very real possibility.

But in the eighth inning the wheels started to come off. Even though he was executing his pitches well, with a high velocity and great location, the first two batters got bloop (a weakly hit fly ball that drops in for a single between an infielder and an outfielder—read: lucky) hits that went over the infielders' gloves for singles. The no-hitter was no longer.

And that's when it happened.

As a sport psychologist, I watch the expressions athletes make as much—and sometimes more—than I do the mechanics of their bodies. I'm looking for any behavior that indicates they are not thinking about themselves or feeling their best. With a pitcher, I start to worry if I see him kicking the dirt on the mound, slumping his shoulders, or lowering his head in between pitches. But in this particular case I noticed that he seemed to be looking incessantly back at the dugout at someone, but I couldn't tell who.

Every time he glanced at the dugout, things got worse with his delivery. He began to hang pitches (allow the pitch to go in a place he didn't want it to go), and before long he had walked two runs in. The manager came to the mound, and he was removed from the game. He kicked the dirt in frustration. He had gone from a no-hitter to a dismal day, and he'd need the bullpen's help to avoid a loss.

After a performance of this type it's typical for the athlete not to want to talk about it with anyone. As part of his job, he has to face an army of reporters thrusting microphones in his face, insisting he explain why and how badly he sucked, over and over again. So the last thing he wants to do is deconstruct his perceived failure one more time with me. For this reason I was surprised when, upon my arrival in the locker room after the game, he beelined toward me. Even more perplexing was the fact that he was laughing as he approached me.

"Fader, you're not gonna freaking believe this!" he said.

And then this player gave me one of the best examples I have ever heard of jumping to conclusions. During that fateful inning he had glanced inadvertently at the dugout in between pitches. Upon doing so he'd noticed that one of his coaches, whom he greatly respected, had a disapproving and critical expression on his face. Compulsively he continued sneaking looks back to the coach, noticing him display increasingly uncomfortable grimaces. Clearly in his mind the coach was unhappy with his performance. As he started second-guessing the pitches he should throw, his concentration was compromised, and his no-hitter was derailed.

After the game he sought out the coach in the clubhouse to discuss his performance. But the coach was nowhere to be found. After ten minutes of searching he found the coach exiting the bathroom.

"Lights out for seven innings—that was awesome! What happened in the eighth?" the coach asked casually.

"Shit, coach, I don't know what happened. I kept looking over at you, and you looked so pissed. It just got in my head a little, I guess."

"What do you mean I looked pissed?"

"I mean, you just kept kinda pacing back and forth and making these expressions like you were mad or something."

The coach broke into a huge laugh and said, "I've had the shits ever since I overdid it on some buffalo chicken wings on the plane last night, and I spent the first part of the game trying to avoid farting a hole in my pants!"

I can't think of a more colorful example of how jumping to conclusions can have a negative impact on us. Here, this talented baseball player was completely locked in and on track. He was pitching the game of his life and feeling good about it. Yet his self-confidence started to crack when he made an incorrect conclusion about his coach's facial expression, assuming it meant the coach was unhappy with him.

He was right. The coach was terribly unhappy. However, it had nothing to do with him.

Jumping to conclusions causes a large majority of the flawed thinking responsible for fear, worry, and lack of self-confidence.

Think of the last time you had to speak in public or were on a date and wondered what the expressions of the people in front of you meant. Did you interpret them positively, negatively, or neutrally? Did you have enough evidence to draw the conclusion you drew?

But before you start judging yourself for jumping to conclusions, it's important you understand that making conclusions, sometimes incorrectly, is based squarely on evolution. For thousands of years our survival as a species depended on it. When we were a group of cave people sitting around a fire and we heard a noise that sounded like a saber-toothed tiger, jumping to the conclusion that it *was* a saber-toothed tiger was necessary for everyone to either grab their spears or run away, just in case. If our ancestors had said, "Oh, it's just the wind" every time, they eventually would all be eaten alive!

Need more proof? Let's return in more detail to the example of the discussion on objective optimism in Chapter 1.

Picture yourself walking down a dark alley late at night in an unfamiliar city. If you see a sweet-looking elderly man with a walker coming toward you, how different is your snap emotional response from what it would be if you saw a muscular guy in a ski mask?

In our day-to-day life there aren't many saber-toothed tigers (or muscular guys in ski masks, thankfully), but our bodies are still hardwired as if there were. So it takes some extra thought and effort to slot our initial cognitive responses into the proper boxes.

When someone doesn't answer a business proposition you've sent them, don't assume it is because they hate it; maybe they are out sick or haven't had a spare moment to catch up on their inbox, or maybe your presentation is sitting in a spam folder. When your teenager starts locking her door when she is in her bedroom, don't jump to the conclusion that she has something bad to hide, like she is doing drugs or sending inappropriate texts to a stranger; it is much more likely that she simply wants privacy. If your boss leaves during the presentation you are giving, don't think it means you are a terrible speaker. Maybe she had to leave early to pick up her kids from school or has a doctor's appointment.

In sports and in life the goal is to figure out how to accurately assess our thoughts about the world and respond appropriately. The more we can check and correct mistakes in the way we perceive ourselves in the world, the stronger and more healthy our self-concept will be—and, in turn, the better our performance will be.

Thinking positively and adaptively doesn't mean ignoring facts or telling yourself things that aren't true. I worked with a talented infielder who was in a long slump. I chatted with him by the batting cage and asked him how I could help. He said, "Doc, I know what you do, I already do it. I tell myself every at-bat that I am going to hit a bomb [home run]."

I had to explain to the player that adaptive self-talk isn't only about being optimistic; we don't have evidence to say that he *will* hit a home run on the next at-bat. Rory McIlroy doesn't tell himself he's going to hole out every shot from every fairway, and Serena Williams doesn't count on acing every single serve. By telling himself that he will certainly hit it out of the park, a player puts himself at risk for disappointment and even lower confidence when he makes an out and fails to prove his statement true. The key is to make self-talk objectively optimistic—that is, based on undeniable truth. We came up with a phrase he could say to himself before every at-bat. Instead of just pumping himself up, the player would say a batting average that he had in previously, "320, 315, or 295," which were all strong batting averages from the previous seasons. By reminding himself of his successful batting averages, he felt more relaxed and able to concentrate on being in the moment. It built natural confidence. This is one of the crucial misunderstandings about positive self-talk. We practice self-statements that are based only on observable, objective facts. If it isn't true, don't say it! Your path to confidence is created by noticing positive things about your performance and abilities, not by inventing facts or hoping for the best.

Speaking of confidence, few jobs in professional sports require more of it than playing guard in the NBA. Alvin Williams played ten seasons in the pros and endured the inevitable streaks and slumps that come with a grueling eighty-two-game season. Alvin told me that when he felt his confidence waver after a rough patch he would remind himself that a cold shooting night or some negative commentary from a coach didn't define who he was. "I would tell myself, 'Al, you know you're good enough,' or I would think about all the players I had played alongside who weren't in the league anymore—and I was." Here Alvin is giving us a sense of what objective optimism is all about. His brain will believe that self-statement, "You're good enough," because he has the evidence of his observation about how many people he outlasted to back it up. You too can find evidence to make your self-talk objective.

Adjustment:
How Objective and Optimistic Is Your Self-Talk?

Before working to make your mantra, it's helpful to assess how optimistic and objective your current self-talk is. Bring to your mind your performance setting. Imagine what you usually say to yourself when you struggle. If you can't easily recollect your self-talk, think of your performance challenge and narrate it as you would a sporting event. Now answer these questions:

> *On a scale of zero to ten, with zero being very negative or pessimistic and ten being the highest possible of optimism, how optimistic is your self-talk?*

> *What evidence do you have for your statements about yourself or your performance?*

If you find that your response to the first question is a number below five, that indicates you're probably not thinking optimistically enough. Similarly, if you can't name the reasons why you are evaluating yourself in the way you are, you are likely not thinking objectively regarding yourself.

But don't worry! At the end of this chapter we will return to work on building you a mantra, a short self-statement that will be optimistic and objective in helping you keep your thoughts as productive as possible.

The way you speak to yourself about your own sub-optimal results will dictate how quickly you recalibrate. Laird Hamilton, the legendary big-wave surfer, operates in a world where misjudging a giant wave can have fatal consequences. He doesn't have time for self-defeating self-talk. "What are you putting in your mind? It's always good to be prepared, but don't prepare for failure because it might become a self-fulfilling prophesy," Hamilton told me. "One time a woman asked me, 'Hey Laird, can you help me with my surfing? Because I really suck . . . ' I said, 'I absolutely can. Repeat after me: *I don't suck. I don't suck. I don't suck. I don't suck.* That's your first surf lesson. Now let's go have fun.'"

Blowing Things out of Proportion

Another client—a star quarterback in the college game and recent NFL draftee—was having a hard time adjusting to the professional game. One of his calling cards was his ability to scramble, but by the fourth game in the season the rookie QB—we'll call him Frank—had been sacked four times in the first quarter. It wasn't unrealistic for Frank to conclude that he had a problem, which is a fair assessment—and one that is necessary to finding a solution.

It isn't helpful to simply think the glass is half full and gloss over important negative information. If the negative conclusion is based on evidence—in this case that Frank was having trouble getting the ball off before defenders sacked him—the focus needs to be on improving our action—through routines, visualization, and all the other techniques we've been discussing.

But after the first sack Frank would say to himself, "Here we go again. I'm going to call a play, have the ball hiked to me, and screw up. So what if I was a star player in college? I'm clearly not cut out for the big time."

In cognitive behavioral therapy we call this *crystal-ball thinking*. Why? In Frank's case one sack and he'd look into his dysfunctional crystal ball to see a future riddled with failure, even though it hadn't happened yet. He'd get more and more anxious, making his problems worse than they already were, and then he would end up fulfilling his own prophesy. His panicked mental state caused him to play indecisively and make more mistakes.

What Frank needed was to learn how to put singular failures—like a sack on a single play—in the right perspective. A negative result doesn't always lead to a bleak future of losing, getting benched, and getting cut. A sack, interception, or strikeout in baseball is what it is. They aren't desired outcomes, but they're small pieces of a much larger game and need to be considered in the proper perspective.

It happens outside of sports as well. Maybe you've been working on a presentation for weeks, but when you get up to give it you mess up the opening lines. For a minute or two you might be thinking you'll never be any good at presentations and that you'll mess up the next one you do too. That kind of thinking will actually make it *more* likely that you'll do just that. You can beat both kinds of flawed thinking—jumping to conclusions and blowing things out of proportion—with some simple strategies and techniques.

The Differences Between Thoughts and Feelings

The first step to improving your *reactions* or your thinking process is to *control the controllables*. Think of the DOT model we discussed in the introductory chapter—Doing, Outcome, and Thinking. We can control what we *do*. And although we cannot control the outcome of what we do, we can control how we *think* about those outcomes.

Simply put, feelings cannot be controlled. Feelings are *outcomes*.

Thoughts, however, can be edited, practiced, and changed. For example, if your goal is to be happier, I can't just tell you, "Don't be sad—everything will be fine."

I mean, I *could* tell you to be happy—although I don't have very much faith that that would be helpful to you. However, I *can* help you identify the thoughts you are having that are leading to you feeling unhappy, and we can work together toward changing that for the better. Thus, the first step in thinking adaptively is to differentiate between thoughts and feelings.

When you catch yourself saying, "I feel like I did a bad job," is that really a feeling?

No! It is a thought. And you can control your thoughts. *Thinking* you did a bad job will make you *feel* bad. So why not think something more positive, as thinking is within your power?

In my practice I've seen countless athletes flourish once they have been able to sort out how the feelings they experience (i.e., sadness, guilt, fear) are different from their thoughts and then work on changing their thoughts for a successful outcome. A very well-known, very large professional football player—we'll call him Clint—once took up two entire cushions on my office couch going through an emotional collapse. He was near tears, talking about a surgery from the year before and now another injury that was threatening to end his long and productive career.

"I feel there is no place for me now," he said. His voice was heavy, and I could feel his loss.

"Is that statement a thought or a feeling?" I asked.

A thought! I encouraged him to elaborate on what he *actually* felt. When we got to the bottom of it, he said he felt hopeless. We returned to examine his thought, that there was no place for him. When evaluating the reality of that statement, he was able to conclude that he finds value in his family and that there were, in fact, many people who had offered him some interesting coaching and front-office opportunities. The more we talked about what could be rewarding in these new roles, the less his feeling of hopelessness dominated him.

We tend to sit with feelings and assume there is nothing we can do about them. That's true: feelings are results. Instead, we need to work on changing our thoughts and actions (D and T of our DOT model) so our feelings (our emotional Outcomes) in turn change. This is as true in sports careers as it is in your own life. The key to beginning your path toward better outcome begins with separating thoughts from feelings.

Feelings are described with emotional words—*sadness, anger, grief, despair, joy, pride, excitement*. Thoughts are meanings or observations we have about situations, people, and things. To prevent jumping to conclusions and blowing things out of proportion, you have to develop a strategy for catching yourself when you start to think something like, "I *feel* like I did a bad job." You have to assess whether that statement is actually true or if it's a generalization or oversimplification.

Friend or Foe?

A long-distance Olympic runner—we'll call her Joan—was transitioning to shorter-distance relay running because of some injury problems, and she was wracked with doubt about it. She wondered whether she would be fast enough. She wondered whether she would be able to gain the respect of the other members of the relay team. And she worried about whether she would have the ability to compete in a team setting when all of her experience and success had previously come through individual efforts.

Before she even started to train for real—and before she had competed in a single event—she had already started to convince herself she was going to (in her words) *suck* as a relay runner.

When you are feeling bad about your performance, the first step is for you to examine your thoughts: What are you thinking that might have led to this bad feeling you have? What makes you think, truly, that you *suck* as a performer, athlete, parent, employee, or entrepreneur?

The next step is to try to argue with yourself, pointing out the flaws in your reasoning. Think about what a friend would say to you about your thought process. Don't just pick any friend: think about a friend who you believe is the most supportive of you and your work, someone who is honest, smart, and positive. If you said, "I *suck*" to them, how would they respond?

Of course, they would disagree. Think about what facts they would point out to illustrate how, in fact, you do not suck. Think precisely about what their answer might sound like.

In Joan's case she worked to find evidence for her ability to sprint and her amazing team skills outside of her marathon running. I asked her how her coach and family would characterize her negative self-assessment. Joan got so into character that she mimicked the southern drawl of her husband, pointing out in his voice how she had won many marathons in a foot race down the stretch, and that she not only managed a host of different difficult type-A parents as president of their local PTA but also participated in a foundation that helped youth in disadvantaged communities.

As good as Clint and Joan had been at their given disciplines over many years, they still fell victim to something with which we all struggle. When you're feeling bad about your performance, you're very susceptible to listening to what I call the "inner foe"—the voice of the loud, critical, judgmental, inner voice in your head that that jumps to negative conclusions and beats you up. Getting caught up in what your inner foe is saying can drag you into a damaging kind of negative feedback loop. You perform badly, and your inner foe tells you that you suck, which hurts your mental performance the next time and causes you to perform badly again.

But ultimately you have control over how you respond to those thoughts.

You decide whether you're going to listen to your inner foe or your inner friend. The more adaptive this conversation, the healthier your "In-Look" will be.

You can fight back by having an internal dialogue with your most supportive friend, who will advocate for you by pointing to the facts—the true evidence—that your foe is wrong.

Here's a blow-by-blow example.

I was working with a big league hitter who had gone twenty at-bats—five games—without a hit. If you watched him on TV, you could see the frustration with each mounting unsuccessful big cut he took with the bat. He'd flip the bat's barrel into his hand and walk, head bowed, back to the dugout. He was a mass of contained rage and resentment. You have to pick your moments when you talk to a player like this. I found that texting has become preferred way for some—especially younger players—to communicate regularly. Here is our text exchange:

"Tough one, bro."
"Tell me about it."
"Regardless of the outcome, what did you think of that last AB?"
"I hit that last ball really hard. Just right to the guy, ya know."
"How hard?"
"Hahahaha . . . he'll be in the training room getting a hand massage."
"No doubt. Why were you looking so twisted up?"
"You know. Just one of those things, it will pass. Just gotta stay positive like you say."
"Right . . . how you gonna do that?"
"You tell me, doc!"
"What were you saying right up to when you went into the box?"

"To be honest, I'm saying, Here we go again . . . please don't do it."

"Yeah . . . so when you are hitting well what are you saying?"

"Nothing really . . . I mean, I'm saying, I'm the Man! Hahaha."

"Right! I know you're half joking, but that's right. . . . Why are you the man?"

"I'm just messing around, doc . . . "

"No . . . seriously, why specifically are you the man?"

"Are you serious?"

"Yes. For once I am . . . "

"Well, they say the ball comes off my bat insanely fast. . . . I hit for a lot of power. I've gone 3 for 4 a bunch of times up here [in the big leagues], so I know I can do it."

"You are right, you and I know you can do it, but you need to remind yourself of that before you go up to hit. If you let your recent results tell you what you should think and not all the stuff that happened before it, you won't show your best stuff."

"You're right. I know I'm here for a reason."

"Yep, you can bet that outfielder's hands on it!"

The result of this text exchange was that this player changed his self-talk from "Oh here we go again" to the mantra of "I know I'm here for a reason." This statement channeled all the evidence he himself had supplied about how and why he will eventually have success. It was this internal messaging that allowed him to get in the correct mind-set to hit.

Every time he hit after that, while walking from the on-deck circle to the batter's box, he would say, "Here for a reason." He would also step out of the box and repeat that mantra whenever he missed a pitch. The result was a big rainfall of extra base hits after his long drought. Having this kind of internal dialogue with yourself and developing what I call a "mantra" will allow you to dramatically improve your "In-Look" and thus develop the most powerful outlook possible.

The Mantra

I've had the honor and pleasure of working with a handful of actors and actresses who operate at or near the one of pinnacle of the dramatic field—winning an Oscar. The physical act of being handed the priceless gold statuette itself isn't a very effective or productive goal for an actor to have because it's an outcome, not a process. Actors are much are more likely to win an Oscar by focusing on things they can control, like the quality and discipline of rehearsing, the selection of good roles, and, perhaps most importantly, building self-confidence.

Like professional athletes, actors have coaches and agents who can help with the business of acting and making the best career decisions. Improving the self-confidence component is where I come in. It would probably surprise you to know that some of the most talented performers you see on the screen go through terrible struggles with confidence.

One of them is a very well-known actress I worked with for the better part of a year—who we'll call Elizabeth. Liz came to me at a point in her life when she was just finishing a high-profile feature film and also going through an equally high-profile—and emotionally rattling—breakup with her boyfriend of five years. Within two meetings Liz embraced the concept of focusing on work, not on the results. Instead of thinking about getting nominated for an Oscar for that recent film or about her ex behaving in a potentially hurtful way, she refocused on what she could do to do things differently and to think about the people and situations in her life in a more positive and adaptive way.

She walked into my New York City office one rainy Wednesday afternoon in heels that made her feel several inches taller than me (and I'm six-foot-one, by the way) and flopped herself on my couch using her oversized sunglasses as a headband to push her blonde highlights out of her way so she could see me better. Without any salutations, our session had begun.

"Can you believe that hooker won an Oscar. . . . All I get is the privilege of being all over the 'who wore it best' shows . . . *story of my life*! I want that fucking Oscar," she said.

"Yup!"

"Yup?! That's all you got for me today, Fader?"

"Actually, I have an Oscar in my drawer. Hold on a second, let me get it for you," I said. We both laughed.

"Right, I know. *Dee—Oh—Tee*," she said. "It isn't about what I am feeling. What am I doing and what am I thinking that'll help me get that Oscar? Right?"

"Sounds like you'd like to begin re-working our plan."

"WHOA! THE. DOCTOR. IS. IN!"

Liz and I went on to discuss her fear of not being nominated for what she perceived to be a masterful performance in her last movie. When I asked her what scared her the most, at first she wasn't able to pinpoint it. But as we talked, I guided her to articulate why it would bother her so much if she weren't nominated. By the end of our conversation she had her real answer: her main fear about not getting the Oscar nomination was that she would feel she "sucked as an actress."

When I introduced the friend/foe idea to her she instantly responded—as most people do—recognizing that she walks around criticizing herself internally a large portion of the day. She told me that inside her head she makes general statements about herself that are negative and "probably not based on the evidence" about what was really going on in her life.

Eager to start, she asked me, "So what should my friend say?"

I told her that although I was willing to be the voice of her friend, it would be much more effective for her to develop her inner "friend" herself and to practice an inner voice she could use in the other 167 hours during her week when she was not meeting with me. The goal of my work with all of my clients—and with you—is not to be the voice that helps them think more adaptively and positively about themselves but to teach them how to think and react in the best way possible in order to lead them down a path toward peak performance and greater enjoyment in life. Making this adjustment stick is like going to the gym. If you go once a week and even meet with a trainer, it will have a positive benefit. But what really matters is all the times that you work out and practice the exercises you have learned in your one hour with the expert. Mental adjustments are similar. The more you practice thinking more adaptively, the more these changes will stick and the more confident and ready to perform you will feel.

So I asked Liz to go back to her terrible feelings about the Oscar and to recount what her thoughts were that led her to feeling terrible.

"I just feel like I'm a terrible actress."

"Aha!" I said. "Is that a *feeling*?"

"No, it's not. You're right. I guess that's a thought."

"Right. It is a thought. What would your closest friend—your smartest ally—say about that thought, that you are a terrible actress?"

"Oh," she said instantly, "she would say that nobody's doing what I'm doing."

When I asked Liz to elaborate, she was able to clearly state specific facts about how her performances on the stage, screen, and television had been recognized by many people as being innovative and worthy of critical attention.

Once Liz had articulated all her "friends'" reasons why she was at the top of her craft, I asked her to come up with a short self-statement—a *mantra*—that she could use to talk to herself—or self-talk—to remind her of this new adaptive, fact-based, and positive way of thinking about herself. The mantra she came up with was inspired by her friends' comments, "I'm doing it differently." Liz began to repeat this mantra to herself whenever she had a negative feeling such as sadness or disappointment around the Oscar experience or any other challenge to her confidence.

Another aspect of the self-talk process that helped Liz was to reorient herself to practicing enjoyment. Over the years she had become so focused on the outcomes. She reported that all she thought about was that gold little man and the accolades she would receive if and when she won it. This overfocus on the endgame took her away from enjoying the moment at hand. We began a weekly check-in to see how and what she enjoyed about her rehearsals and stage performances. At the end of each work day Liz began the habit of asking herself, "What did I enjoy most about that?" At first it was difficult for her to find enjoyment in some aspects of her creative work. But in time she didn't even have to prompt herself by asking the question. At the conclusion of shooting each scene or while walking back to her dressing room, she would simply say to herself, "I enjoyed _____ about that performance." This "enjoyment self-talk" was very effective in helping her have a process focus and perform at her best, thus improving her chances that she would eventually achieve her desired outcome.

Yuri Foreman, former WBA super welterweight champion, told me in detail about his mantras:

When you go into the ring, it's exciting but scary, and that is because much of what will happen is unknown and outside your control. I work to completely mute out the negative thoughts. Boxing training is rooted in repetition. You repeat punches and physical sequences, and you must repeat mantras to keep yourself mentally strong. When I'm preparing for a fight, I have certain self-statements that I believe in to help me get myself ready for battle. Mantras like "I've trained hard," "I've done all the hard work," "I'm ready," "Whatever he brings, I can handle it," "The universe will protect me." Repeating these mantras keeps me confident and ready.

Another one of the most effective mantras I've heard from an athlete came from Rennae Stubbs. A tall, agile player with a terrific net game, she would still sometimes feel some self-doubt before a big match against a talented doubles team. But she told me that her mantra, "Do what you do," reminded her that she was the intimidator at the net and that she deserved to be on the court. "It comes down to knowing the things you're really good at, whether it's on the court or in life," Stubbs said. "Don't let the thoughts about what you *can't* do prevent you from doing the things you *can* do." What was most powerful about Rennae's mantra was that it was objectively optimistic. Her mantra didn't promise her a first-place finish or a dramatic win. It was simple, centering, and based on evidence. She had abilities, and they had come out in the past. Her self-talk was simply there to remind her of her capabilities and summon her confidence in them.

A mantra can be seen as a tool to actively work on changing your story. Maybe for you it involves your worth as a parent: "I work as hard for my children as I have ever worked for anything in my life." Or maybe it addresses your work insecurities: "My review said I am responsible and creative." Or, for example, the baseball player's mantra of his batting average, "315." The mantra—or short, data-based, positive self-statement—is like a pen with which you can actually begin to cross out and rewrite particularly unhelpful ways of perceiving yourself and your environment. Using the mantra above, Liz, along with hundreds of other athletes and performers I've worked with, have been able to rewrite, edit, and reframe the "story of their life" in their minds. And so can you. It is amazing how something that seems so simple and straightforward has such a strong power to help better your life.

As a model for how mantras can look, here is a list of mantras from people in different walks of life I have worked with:

Law enforcement officer: "Honor comes from my focus."

Actor: "Broadway welcomed me."

Parent: "Listen well—lead well."

Hockey player: "In my calm. I am relentless."

CEO: "My power comes from my struggle."

Basketball player: "Started at the bottom."

PhD student: "I'll do my best 'cause my best is all I can do."

Author of this book: "Just this moment."

The So-Called Law of Attraction

Be mindful not to mix up the idea of the personal mantra with the Law of Attraction—perhaps one of the most prevalent ideas in many self-help books designed to help you change your life today. This idea basically says that by directing our thinking to positive thoughts or outcomes, we will increase the likelihood of those things coming true. A best-selling and popular example of a book that employs a like-minded theory is Napoleon Hill's *Think and Grow Rich*.[4] This idea was also popularized in the movie and book *The Secret*.

Sounds great, obviously.

But do you really think that if you believe hard enough that you will live a life filled with success, fulfillment, and riches and that your sheer thought process will make it happen?

An attractive proposition, and one that sold many books as a result. But it has some pretty serious problems. There isn't a direct relationship between simply thinking positively about the future in a non-evidenced-based way and an outcome.

No, you can't become rich by thinking you are going to be rich. But the so-called Law of Attraction does have its uses, in everything from sports to wealth accumulation. One of my professional basketball clients—we'll call him Jimmy—would sometimes rip into himself and say he was a terrible free-throw shooter. He wasn't. We worked together to examine the evidence, which showed that he was about average for players with his time in the game. But after he missed the first shot, he would say to himself, "I suck at free throws." Predictably, he would miss his second shot when he did this.

It isn't magic that causes this decline in performance. When you think these negative thoughts, it informs your actions. Jimmy told himself to fail. Because he did this, he diminished his concentration, raised his heart rate, and actually behaved differently. If you change your message to yourself, you change the way you act, and thus, your results change. When Jimmy was able to counter these thoughts and develop a positive mantra, "Just this shot," it helped him change the way he approached each free throw, and then his result changed.

This concept has applications to all sorts of everyday problems and challenges. Whenever we drive home to our apartment in New York City, my wife and I play the Law of Attraction parking game. It is hard to find a parking place in our urban neighborhood. So we envision the parking space and assume we are going to find it. Does that magically create the parking space? No! Of course not!

But consider this: *by assuming we will find it, our behaviors change.* We are looking at every small space as one we might fit into, not as one that won't work. We are looking at every space close to a fire hydrant as possibly being far enough away rather than ruling it out as too close. When there is a big event at a nearby theater, we don't let it affect our objective optimism about our ability to find a space; instead, it keeps our spirits high, even as we drive in circles. We arrive home without feeling frazzled. We then are able to greet our children with the same good mood. Our behavior rubs off on them, and they go to bed more cheerily. We all sleep better, and in the morning I start my job refreshed. In small ways and large, I believe this optimistic orientation leads to behaviors that can help you actually achieve your *goals* and change your life. If you change your "story," your behaviors change and, thus, so does your life.

Many people talk to me about wanting to find success at work or love. In applying the Law of Attraction here, it's unhelpful to believe that just having positive self-talk about these things will lead to them happening. But believing you will find love or that you will be successful at work will change every interaction you have with every date and professional opportunity. Every bar you walk into *might* contain your life partner, and that positive outlook will affect the sort of persona you project and, thus, increase your chances of finding what you are looking for.

Fans look at athletes with a sense of awe over their moments of brilliance and in disbelief at the times when they come up short. How do they rise to greatness in situations where it seems humanly impossible, and why do they fail in others that seem clearly within their grasp? The answer is in the secrets of their thoughts. Athletes who work to train their thinking and self-talk to be positive and adaptive are able to bounce back from setbacks and to reach most deeply into their well of talent to retrieve their very best. By using concepts from this chapter to recognize and change your negative thinking, along with some continued practice, you will be able to do the same.

What at first will be difficult—changing the inner voice in yourself from negative to that of your most positive friend—takes adjustment and work, but the rewards of that change are significant. The inner voice of a professional athlete allows him or her to proceed with confidence through their accomplishments—and it will allow you better chances to succeed in your work and in your personal life.

How-To—Make Your Mantra

When I talk about the concept of establishing a mantra to some of the athletes in my practice, I occasionally see some initial hesitation. They think I'm either going to hit them with something "new agey" and cheesy or drop something heavy and scientific on them.

Making a mantra is actually neither of those things. It's something you can—and should—do yourself. It works as a calming, simplifying thought you use to yourself to reinforce a positive, *accurate* inner monologue.

A good mantra is short, simple, prescriptive, and, most importantly, specific.

If your goal is to improve your parenting and to short-circuit negative thinking within that arena, it isn't useful to have "I'm a good dad" as your mantra. It needs to have a very specific, accurate component: "I'm a good dad because I make the commitment to put the girls to bed at least two nights a week." To equate it with something in the sports realm, a baseball hitter shouldn't just be saying "I'm the best hitter"; the statement needs to be something like "I hit .305 last year. I deserve to be here." These longer statements can then be shortened to something more portable like "Committed to the everyday" for the parent or, in the case of the baseball player, "Deserve it."

The beauty of mantras is that—unlike tattoos—they don't have to be permanent. You can—and should—change them regularly to make sure they suit your current situation, and you should absolutely experiment with a few different ones when you're starting this exercise for the first time. A good mantra will not only be authentic to you, but it will also *feel* authentic. As you say it to yourself during a bout with negative thoughts, you won't get distracted by any disconnect between the content of the mantra and the ultimate truth of the words behind it. It won't do you any good to say to yourself, "I'm the best saleswoman in North America" if you know it isn't true. It's far more useful to say "I outwork everybody in my division, and no client will ever have a shortage of information."

Here are some questions to ask yourself to help you find your mantra:

What are the qualities that make me good at what I am trying to accomplish?

What is the evidence or facts that prove my ability in this area?

What do my close friends, confidants, coaches, mentors, family, and bosses say about my strengths in this area?

What is a phrase that describes these strengths about me as written above?

Now test yourself. Using a percentage, how much do you believe the sentence you have written? If it's less than 75 percent, then see if you can change your mantra to be more fact based. Think of the undeniable reasons that prove your ability or skill in the area in which you are trying to improve. Write your refined mantra below:

It helps to reinforce your mantra by making it part of your daily pre-, during-, and postperformance routine. Keep this in mind as you read the next chapter on routines. You can strengthen its power by saying it when you wake up and when you go to bed. Also, it is helpful to post your mantra in a place where you can see it. Many athletes put their mantra on their cell phone lock screen, computer monitor, or bathroom mirror. I've worked with executives who print out a fortune-cookie-size mantra and put it on their office phone or tape a giant-print version to their window. Any place you see it, it will be a reminder to train your brain to think in an objectively optimistic way. One universal Life as Sport mantra is "Stay on the DOT." In stressful moments this mantra will help you focus on the process of things you can control.

When I work with elite performers I frequently ask them in our first meeting, "Who are the most important people you speak to during a typical day?" Almost instantly they say their wives, husbands, parents, and kids. I wait. Puzzled, they look at me, and almost as a question, they offer other answers: "My coach?" "Agent?" "You!?" Finally, most figure it out. Themselves! *You* are the most important person you speak to every day. *Your* messages, in the form of self-statements or self-talk, inform how you feel about yourself and, thus, impact your performance. By practicing the techniques in this chapter you will have healthier, more productive conversations with yourself inside of your head, and thus, you will perform at your best.

Enjoyment Exercise

Mantra swap. Explain the idea of self-talk and a mantra to a friend or coworker. Describe what you're trying to change about your outlook to each other. Come up with a mantra for your friend, and have your friend do the same. Share the mantras and collaborate to make them more personalized and effective. Once a week e-mail your friend a reminder of her mantra and have her do the same for you.

7

Set Routines to Win the Game Before It Begins

You wake up one morning in the dead of winter and you're freezing, but you can't figure out why. You hop out of bed and realize that you left the window in your bedroom wide open all night. As you make your way to the bathroom, you see that you left a bunch of other windows open too. You'll deal with the windows in a second, but first you need to use the bathroom—but you can't because the toilet overflowed and flooded everything. You decide to go to the gym and shower before work, but you open your closet and don't have any clean clothes. When you pick up your phone to call the dry cleaners, you see that you forgot to charge it. All of a sudden your growling stomach reminds you that you haven't eaten anything since six last night. However, when you open your usually overstocked fridge, you find it empty, aside from a forlorn, decaying avocado. Guess it's time to drive to the deli for breakfast instead. But when you go to pick up your car keys from the bowl by the door, they aren't there. You see your wallet on the table—thankfully—but when you open it, you discover that it's empty!

Is this all a bad dream?

I certainly hope so!

It is a scenario that is highly unlikely to happen in real life because most humans operate on a series of routines. We all build systems that almost become automatic, and they're designed to address the issues we face every day. They're standardized plans for the activities you engage in daily. Some people handle things pretty well from day-to-day with good routines. Other people have a little more trouble. But even if you fancy yourself as somebody with a terrific day-to-day plan, there's a big difference between managing the everyday and moving toward our goal in this book: experiencing peak performance in your life.

When you think about your ultimate performance goals—whether it's playing a sport at the highest level, making a presentation that leads to a big sale, developing an important personal relationship, or anything else—you probably don't have a particularly well-planned set of routines to put you in the most prepared mental state to achieve them. Most of us have trained our whole lives to execute the next day very well. You put out your clothes for the next day, make sure you have enough cash on hand for the day, stock your fridge for the next few meals, and so forth. But very few of us have developed the right plan for long-range, high-level peak performance through improved, streamlined mental processes.

You likely don't have a well-designed, well-aimed mental routine.

In this chapter I'll show you what elite athletes and business people do to conceive, establish, and follow the mental routines that separate the highest achievers from the rest of the pack. The techniques we'll discuss are ones you can integrate into your plan immediately, on day one.

Yuri Foreman, boxer and former WBA super welterweight champion, talked with me about how important routines are at boosting confidence:

> When it comes down to it, boxing is rather mechanical. Preparing in the gym and having a routine helped me to be confident in the ring. If I stuck to my training routine in the gym, I was more confident. But when it comes time to fight, your mental preparation is what allows your physical preparation to really shine. All my physical preparation helps me to control my thoughts. When I knew I was prepared, I had more positive thoughts. Just like in the rest of life, thinking positively, within reason, was essential for a good result in the ring. If you have a negative thought, don't complain if your results are negative.

What Is a Routine?

When you watch a top-ranked professional golfer, major league hitter, pro quarterback, or other elite athlete, you'll probably notice regular "rituals" they follow before and during competition. PGA Tour player Jason Day goes through an extremely precise mental and physical routine before he hits every shot, and it can be timed down to the second. It starts when he pulls the club from his bag, involves preparing mentally and physically to hit the shot, and includes a visualization component. He immerses himself so deeply in his routine that he pushes out most of the mental and emotional "static" in the background that could cause him anxiety and distract him from peak performance.[1]

Former NFL player Mike Robinson has carried over his morning routine from his playing days right through to his time as an announcer for the NFL Network. He gets up and immediately cues some of his favorite music and plays it loudly as he starts to get ready. "Fader, I look in the mirror, and I get into what I call my 'superman' pose," Mike told me once with a chuckle. "I stand there like I'm on top of the world, and I sing my song and get my head together for the day. I do it every single day. If you start your day like you're down or like it's going to be a bad day, how can you be surprised when that actually happens?" Mike also told me that he noticed that his kids imitate him, thus transmitting how he practices this confidence-building routine through modeling.

NFL quarterback Peyton Manning has become legendary for the routine he established for the twenty-four hours leading up to a game—from dissecting film to inspecting game balls to quizzing his receivers to make sure they're ready for what's about to happen. By definition a routine is a series of mental and physical behaviors that allow you to bring your best self to a given situation.[2] The beauty—and complexity—of a routine is that it can consist of any action that performs one of two key functions: it can involve something physical, such as an exercise that slows down your breathing as discussed in Chapter 4 on anxiety management, or it can be something that changes how you think about the situation, like a mantra or adaptive self-talk statement, as in Chapter 6. Both allow you to be more focused in your big moment. Regardless of whether we're discussing the physical or mental components of routine, either one helps you feel more in control of your surroundings and more immune to the stimuli around you that can interfere with your performance.

As we discussed in the last chapter, coaches often tell their players to "slow down" or "focus." A routine is a method to actually reach these goals by allowing you to block out irrelevant information. When you practice your routine with enough repetition that it becomes automatic, it will allow you to be present in the moment and shield you from thoughts and results that are beyond your control. Just as a well-designed mental routine works for big leaguers in big moments, it will work for you in your presentation, performance, or other important situation.

Many years ago one of my baseball clients told me about a game where he experienced the "golden sombrero"—striking out all four times he came to bat in a game. When we connected on the phone there were no pleasantries to kick off the conversation, no "how's the family?" kind of stuff.

"Thinking is fucking horrible," he grunted.

As crude as that may sound, it's really what we're talking about here.

One of the purposes of sport and performance psychology in general and establishing a routine in particular is to help performers learn how to perform without thinking—specifically, allowing us to perform without being overwhelmed by thoughts and emotions. That sounds nice, of course, but how exactly does that work? After all, if I suggest to you that you shouldn't think about a shiny black briefcase full of money, what happens the moment you hear that request?

Don't worry. You can't help it. The image of a shiny black briefcase full of money probably appeared in your mind. In fact, most people are wired in a persistent, paradoxical, and frustrating way. When it is suggested to them that they shouldn't think about something, it actually makes them think about it more. For most of us it's equally problematic to hear that we should try not to think about anything. By trying to create a blank space, so to speak, all we really do is open the door to distracting thoughts.

By focusing on a mental and physical behavioral routine, you're giving your mind a very specific, focused task. The act of following those mental and physical assignments keeps your mind protected from the unhelpful distractions that make high-level achievement so difficult.

What does it feel like? Try this exercise.

Put this book down and get yourself into as relaxed a state as possible. Choose your own way to completely let go. Use whatever strategy you've tried in the past to fully relax your mind, body, and spirit. Come on! Give it a shot . . .

Are you back?

If you're like me—and most people—you probably picked some combination of closing your eyes, relaxing your muscles, or even lying down on a couch. Some of you might have taken it a step farther and re-created in your mind a relaxed scene you've either experienced yourself or dream about, like going to a beach. These are all naturally ingrained, reflexive routines we default to when we try to relax. Maybe you even used the breathing techniques you learned in Chapter 4.

When you build your own routine, you're drawing on the behavioral responses built into all of us to make a more elaborate, consistent, and reliable relaxation response. You're creating a deliberate mental and emotional plan to prepare yourself to perform at a peak level. There's no doubt your mind can be trained to produce specific, productive thoughts in a given situation. We are in a successful routine when we establish what those thoughts and actions are ahead of time and come up with a plan to prompt them.

All that's left afterward is to actually perform the routine itself. That might seem self-evident, but it's important to mention because it's the step most people gloss over when they undertake a plan to build a routine. You don't get the benefit of having a routine unless you actually do the underlying work to establish the routine as a habit and then actually do it until it becomes ingrained.

And it's something you have to work toward doing every time you perform.

Routines vs. Superstitions

Before we build your routine, let's differentiate between an effective routine and superstition. Years ago Boston Red Sox third baseman Wade Boggs became famous for both his ability to hit for a high batting average and for the seemingly eccentric pregame rituals he followed down to the letter. According to firsthand reports, he would start by eating the same chicken dish before heading to the field (his wife was rumored to have dozens of chicken recipes by the end of his career). Once he got there, he would field exactly 150 balls from his position, and before an 8 p.m. night game he would start his batting practice at exactly 5:27 p.m. Then he'd run a set of wind sprints down the foul line at exactly 7:17 p.m. It might sound eccentric, but what Boggs was doing was creating order in his mind-set by taking away as many mental variables as he could so that he could focus all of his attention on the task at hand.[3]

Serena Williams has mentioned the same kind of superstitious preparation for her tennis matches. When she lost in the third round of the 2008 French Open her first comment in the postmatch interview was that she felt "off" because she hadn't gone through her normal pattern before playing: "I didn't tie my laces right. I didn't bring my shower sandals to the court with me. I didn't have my extra dress. I knew it wasn't going to happen."[4]

Superstitious sports rituals like Boggs's and Williams's came about years before sport psychology and mental-skills training was huge in elite sports because athletes interpreted the superstitions as being the cause for improved performance. The increased control and focus they felt as a by-product of religiously following the superstitious behavior made them believe that the superstition itself—eating the same meal, going through the same activity pattern—was the determining factor.

Groundbreaking psychologist B. F. Skinner established much of what we know about human behavior through a series of studies at Harvard in the 1950s and 1960s. One of his studies clearly illustrated this concept of superstitious reinforcement. Pigeons in cages received food in regular intervals unrelated to the birds' behavior. The pigeons learned to associate the delivery of that food with whatever activity they happened to be performing when the food came, so they kept performing that action, even when it didn't result in more food delivery.[5]

In this case, anyway, we're not so different from pigeons.

We're all trying to connect our actions with rewards and do more of the things that produce more rewards. And clearly some athletes do benefit from participating in "superstitious" behavior, even if the superstitious behavior isn't necessarily the true cause of the improved performance. But our goal here is to create a system of routines that not only fill the control and anti-anxiety roles served by some of that superstitious behavior but also offer real behavioral benefits in their own right.

Take Wade Boggs's obsession with eating chicken. In his head it worked for him, but the reality is that the kind of chicken you eat doesn't truly impact performance directly. Also, what happened if the chicken he wanted wasn't available? In a more productive routine players have that same focus through a breathing technique that has actual, quantifiably positive physical and mental benefits. It's a ritual, but one that's authentically good for your performance.

As long as a superstition doesn't harm your performance, it is usually neutral or positive. However, some superstitions can interfere with your actual performance, as was the case of the famed story of soccer star Kolo Touré. Touré had a superstition, the solid belief that he needed to be the last person onto the field coming back from halftime. In one game one of his teammates was injured and didn't come out right away, but Touré insisted on waiting, and it forced his team to start the second half short two players![6]

Does that mean Serena Williams should stop bringing her shower shoes to a match or that you should get rid of the lucky socks you wear every time you have a big presentation? Absolutely not. A good routine can be a mix of superstition and "real" preparation.

Take Stefan Holm, an elite Swedish high jumper. In his preparation he would always read volumes of material about the location of his next competition. If he knew he was going to be jumping over a bar set at 225 centimeters, he would make sure to read at least 240 pages of material beforehand so he would have the higher number set in his mind. Just before performing he would go through a more traditional physical and mental routine that included secluding himself and visualizing his upcoming performance. During the competition he followed a series of superstitions like eating only corn flakes and orange juice, showering twice, and packing his bag in the same order. He would wear the same underwear to every meet and would religiously put his right sock and left shoe on first.[7]

A good bit of Holm's routine was based on superstition, but at the core he used many of the techniques we've been talking about in this book to prepare. The superstitious part (i.e., order of dressing, eating a particular food) didn't get in the way of the "real" preparation (i.e., mentally rehearsing information about the location of the competition, visualizing his performance, etc.), as these routines are actually tied causally to a process that impacts the results. They are thoughts and behaviors (D and T of DOT) that affect the outcome. Our goal is to build a mental and physical routine into your daily life that fundamentally improves your performance in critical areas but isn't tied together with the "magic string" of a superstition.

Peak-Performance Routine Templates

When I talk to my business clients about the concept of routines, the first thing they usually ask is whether a routine adapted from baseball or any other sport is similar enough to what a "regular person" would need to use in the business world.

In other words, does a sport like baseball require such a specialized collection of skills that it makes for a bad template to generalize routines into business and other settings? In my experience the answer is an emphatic "no." As you probably gathered from the title of this book, *Life as Sport*, I believe life is a series of performances. Every day is an at-bat, a new game with which opportunity is present. It's one big chance to be present, enjoy things, and try to compete with yourself to be the best version of yourself in each moment. I use the same methods for building routines to help physicians perform their medical procedures more efficiently as I do to help an infielder improve the accuracy of his fielding. Both of those people are "performing" in the literal sense of the word. There may or may not be an audience of forty thousand involved when you're a surgeon or salesperson, but both jobs require a collection of skills and experience that need to combine in complex ways to produce the best possible result. And both jobs require the performer to think optimally.

Maybe you're sitting there thinking that the supposedly elaborate process of building a routine is fine for a baseball player making millions of dollars, who goes up to the plate with the World Series on the line, but that it isn't "worth it" for somebody with a basic everyday business problem to solve.

I can tell you that I've had the opportunity to collaborate with the members of specialized military and law enforcement training groups, and you won't find another collection of people who go to work with more on the line. They have taught me a ton about performance psychology—and the consequences of getting it right or wrong with human lives in the balance. When I share some of these ideas with my elite athletic clients, they often say the same thing: all they're doing is hitting a ball, which is nothing compared to being on an actual battlefield or climbing a ladder to go fight a fire.

For me it's all just a matter of scale.

The same positive and centering routines that help Navy SEALs perform at their peak also help a baseball player be better prepared and will make you be your best self in a meeting. You can improve your enjoyment and success at any meaningful action in your life—at work, at play, at home—by paying closer attention to how you think and how you manage the triggers those actions produce. By going into any complex action with a routine and a plan, you're giving yourself a much greater chance of not only completing the action successfully but also being able to manage the situation if something less-than-ideal happens.

What does this look like at the elite level?

In sports many athletes have a variety of routines and use them depending on the situation. They usually have preperformance routines for the day before or day of competition and then a preperformance routine for the minutes just before actually competing. Former NBA player John Amaechi described to me his somewhat unorthodox routine of making and drinking tea with milk (he's British) on the bench after warm-up and before a game, which let him reconnect to the emotions of the upcoming game in a more productive way and focus his attention on something calming.

"I had a routine—perhaps because I'm British—of drinking tea before each game," John shared with me. "I became well known by my teammates for sitting on the bench after my warm-up and drinking tea with milk. This was before everybody was talking about mindfulness. I sat there and was able to separate myself from all of my worldly experience. As I drank my tea, I just let my focus drift toward my moment with this hot beverage and was able to separate from the emotions surrounding the upcoming game. I remember one big game against New York when I got too caught up in the possible outcomes of the game—my teammates noticed me sitting on the bench biting my fingernails and came over to ask me why I wasn't doing my normal tea routine. It became clear to me that this ritual had taken on meaning for them, as it had for me, and this was in some way a psychological sign that everything was okay—we had cleanly separated from the stress of preparing to go to battle and were ready to compete."

John went on to further stress the importance of a routine that helps you have a process focus: "In playing in the NBA, I found myself to be an average player. I needed to work hard to have success. In that, I found that enjoying things was sometimes outside of my grasp—but I did focus on contentment. My main source of contentment was feeling like I had a really good process. Regardless of whether I was playing or not or had objective success, if I looked back on my performance, I could say that I focused on the process and excelled in that. Because of that, I felt very content about my playing."

Players also have another routine to use during the game itself—say, during the shooting of a free throw or hitting a shot on the golf course. Many also have postperformance routines designed to help metabolize and integrate information and emotion from what they just experienced and use it to inform the next competition. The elements of the routine you establish will vary depending on what part of the performance the routine is for. To prepare you to perform, you want to use different tools from those you would use to calm down and synthesize what happened after the fact.

For example, one of my financial clients developed a well-oiled combination of routines for a sales call that involved breathing and positive self-statements beforehand, focus on composure, facial expressions and posture during the meeting, and reviewing her observations to make sure they were evidence based and that her self-talk remained healthy after the meeting had concluded.

For one veteran baseball pitcher who has been a longtime client, routine has become a crucial part of how he handles a negative outcome on the field. He was always a very composed guy, even long before we started to work together. Then, one day at a meeting, he described to me how he helped younger pitchers replicate his "triage" routine. "Whenever I get rocked and somebody hit one out," he told me, "I get the new ball back from the umpire or catcher, and I concentrate on rotating it in my glove while reciting the alphabet backward. I pay attention to the texture of the seams, and that helps me breathe right and stay in the moment so I can give my complete attention to the next pitch."

And that's one of the big-picture goals of any routine—helping you "normalize" or "optimize" as much as possible before, during, and after performing. I use the term "normalize" because so much of performance has to do with regulating intensity and arousal. Contrary to what you might hear in a television broadcast, all of those things aren't necessarily bad. You need a certain level of intensity and arousal to feel in the moment and have the energy and motivation to perform.

The problems come when you're at one of the ends of the meter on either side. If you're too intense or aroused, you'll tend to have a lot of anxiety and will be prone to the bad decision making that comes from your circuits being "overloaded." The opposite end of the scale is just as much of a problem: if you aren't intense or aroused, you will tend to show a low energy level or some disengagement and listlessness. This is where your routine comes in; it helps you to stay even and present in these big moments.

The specific building blocks you use for your routines are up to you, but the pattern you make with them will resemble many of the chapter headings in this book. The routine becomes a way to bring together the different components of performance psychology.

For example, in the chapter on motivation you identified the Power Value that inspires you to achieve your goal. One part of a pre-performance routine related to motivation could involve finding a quiet place to go with an iPod and headphones and listen to a collection of two or three songs that capture the essence of your intrinsic motivation and enjoyment of the activity you're about to undertake. For an athlete, motivation might come from the sense that it's an opportunity to show what he or she can really do, and some particular song intensifies the feelings that come from that desire.

Translated into the everyday world of business, one sales professional I worked with came to me after a series of subpar results.

We came up with pre- and postperformance routines that allowed her to change her focus to more positive things. In her pre-performance routine she listened to some music and repeatedly reminded herself that her drive to be creative and to set a good example for her niece were her main motivations to stay strong in the harsh environment of corporate sales. In her post-performance routine she was able to review each meeting she had and point out which aspect of it she enjoyed, regardless of the result. She wrote down something she was grateful for about each day in sales. This helped her put outcomes in perspective, as it always left her thankful that she had the opportunity to compete. She then reminded herself about the moments she was at her best and resolved to replicate more of those moments in the next meeting.

In Chapter 4 we focused on managing anxiety. Some routines are designed to help performers handle anxiety in a more adaptive way. During a tense trading period on the stock exchange, a trader might default to an in-performance routine that repeats a self-statement that focuses him. One trader I worked with would combine a centering breath with the words "one trade" to remind himself to focus on one trade at a time. This combination of relaxation techniques with self-talk was the ideal mixture to build an effective in-performance routine to help him to be more present and perform at his best.

The actual mechanism for the routine—whether it's listening to a particular song, immersing yourself in a certain game on your iPhone, or stretching in your office before an important call—isn't as important as the overall act of doing a routine in general. It can be as simple as taking the How-To exercises at the end of each of the chapters in this book, breaking them down into small, simple pieces, and practicing one of them at a given time. Over time the ritual of doing it will create a powerful ingrained response. You're literally changing the way you think and act to respond with greater presence and focus in high-stakes situations.

Micro-Failures:
Shrinking Mistakes with Resetting Routines

Before we finish with an exercise that will help you perfect your routine-building process, let's talk about the most common roadblocks that could get in your way as you get started. The biggest setbacks are usually due to failing to establish the routine as a habit and getting pushed out of your routine in a high-pressure situation.

Building the habit of using a routine is just like building any other habit: the more you're able to integrate the habit into your daily life, the easier it will be. If the routine you build is elaborate, time consuming, and hard to follow without a reference card, it's going to be more difficult to follow than one that has a few simple cues and thoughts or actions. It's also important to remember that routines work when they're used regularly, but it isn't a zero-sum game; not using your routine one time doesn't mean that you're a failure and that using it the next time is a waste of time. I like to think of it the same way a baseball player thinks about his fielding percentage: the goal is to not commit any errors, but when you make an error it doesn't mean you give up on the rest of the balls hit your way; it means you're trying to be error-free on all the balls to come!

Watch any high-level sporting event this week and you'll see athletes getting pushed out of a routine. Quarterbacks will get hounded into making bad throws. With a strike or two against them, batters will swing and miss at pitches they should have let go. Players at the highest level—who have the most solid routines—still make mistakes. They still get discouraged and succumb to the pressure of the moment. Perfection isn't possible. The only goal here is to create a system and a plan to have the best chance at peak performance. We talked about it earlier in the chapter, when Serena Williams lamented the fact that she didn't follow her routine before a match.

So how do you keep that from happening? Or if you're following your routine, how do you keep it from deteriorating under pressure? Take the person who has to give a presentation at a sales conference. If she gives the presentation and gets a less-than-favorable response from an audience member, it's completely natural to react negatively to that experience.

Baseball is a game of adjustments. Many coaches will say that the best baseball players know how to put the last error, hit, or strikeout behind them and move on to the next opportunity. San Francisco Giants player Matt Duffy wrote something very revealing in the online magazine the *Players Tribune*: "I'd watch Buster [Posey] strike out in a big situation, and come back to the dugout—never cursing or throwing stuff, remaining as cool as could be. And I'd learn a lot from that: about just how much failure—and dealing with failure—is part of Major League Baseball. About how preparation, and not outcome, is what a smart player will focus on. Buster accepted his micro-failures and moved on to the next at-bat. If the best guy on the team can do that, how can't I?"[8]

Here Duffy is calling back to our DOT model of focusing on the process and not the outcome, but more importantly he is talking about how a veteran like Buster Posey can quickly move on from a minor bad outcome, or what he refers to as a "micro-failure." This is the exact term I use with athletes and peak performers in all areas. A micro-failure is a small incident or situation that occurs during your performance that, though not ideal, will not mean your defeat in the game or meeting as long as you are able to move on and get back to your game plan.

One of your best weapons against the micro-failure is an in-game (or in-meeting, in-performance, in-discussion) resetting routine. A resetting routine is exactly what it sounds like: a series of actions or thoughts that allows you to flush away the minor micro-failure, reset, and get back on track. One of my colleagues and forerunners in the field of sport psychology, Ken Ravizza, who now works with the Chicago Cubs, is famous for putting a toilet in the clubhouse for a baseball team to really "flush" their micro-failures![9]

I have worked with performers in many different settings to engineer effective resetting routines. Recently I worked with a young chess prodigy who was competing against adults on a world stage. When playing opponents who were rated higher than him, he was usually relaxed and locked in mentally. But when facing off against an opponent whom he should dominate, he sometimes faltered. This was especially true if he made a mistake like giving up a minor piece—a pawn, for example—in the early stage of the game. This type of micro-failure would lead to diminished focus, and he would frequently make a string of errors that ultimately led to his defeat. Together we designed a routine for him to practice directly after a micro-failure in a game. If he made a mistake, he would take off his glasses, shut his eyes for a second, take a centering breath (remember Chapter 4), and repeat a mantra designed for his in-game resetting routine: "focus on what I can control" or "next move." This resetting routine helped him get back on track and play his best game, no matter what small obstacles he faced during the game. When he put his glasses on a couple of seconds later, he was refreshed, back to his mental starting point, and ready to win again.

How-To: Building Your Routine

When I'm talking to baseball players about this exact subject, we'll start by working backward. I'll ask them, "How do you want to feel when you step into the batter's box?" The answer is usually, "I want to feel loose and ready." Now, what are the things we can do in a routine that will give you the best chance to feel that way—and if you don't feel that way, what are the things that are most likely to trigger the negative reaction?

In baseball a pitcher might have trouble with a hitter he knows "owns" him, meaning that batter has had a lot of lifetime success against him. When that hitter comes up it might mean that the pitcher loses confidence in what he does and starts guiding the ball, or he gives in and essentially avoids the confrontation by "pitching around the batter"—throwing off the plate. A better routine would involve self-talk that reminds the pitcher he's on a major league roster for a reason and reinforces the scouting report the team made on that hitter before the game. "If I throw my pitch low and away, I've done my job. If he does something great with it, I tip my cap and move on." In time and with practice this self-talk might be reduced to "low and away" or "just this pitch."

You've probably noticed that a big component of both of these solutions is positivity—and reframing a situation so you embrace it and learn from it. That goes to the core of what I believe *Life as Sport* is: a way of learning to perform at your best *and, at the same time,* to enjoy the experience no matter what your results are. We are always looking for a way to be objectively optimistic. This is different from saying that we "will win" or "hope we win." Being objectively optimistic in our routines and thoughts is about focusing on noticing the facts we can observe about why we are great. The more we incorporate into our routines our observations about how we are capable and lucky to have the talents and experiences we have, the more we will play at our best, thus creating more evidence for our talents.

Few athletes personify this concept more completely than retired professional tennis player Rennae Stubbs. One of the greatest doubles players in the history of the women's game, she won four Grand Slam women's doubles titles and two Grand Slam mixed doubles titles, and she competed in four Olympics for her native Australia. In all my discussions with Rennae I have found her to be unique in her understanding of how lessons learned on the tennis court can apply to life. She was always aware of how her mind-set impacted her tennis performance.

Early in her career Stubbs was playing in a women's doubles semifinal match when she became incensed with what she thought was a dishonest move by one of her opponents. At a crucial moment in the match, Stubbs was so distracted by her anger at what happened that she tried to hit the woman across the net with a shot. Stubbs's team would go on to lose the match, costing Stubbs a chance at the one Grand Slam she would end up not winning.

"Jonathan," she said with a thoughtful pause, "I let my emotion get the better of me there, and it escalated and cost us a game," Rennae told me, who won the 2001 world doubles championship with Lisa Raymond. "We ended up losing that set and the match. After it was over I promised myself I would never let my emotions get out of control like that again. It was a pivotal point in my career. I learned a huge lesson, which is that you have to take all of the positive *and* negative things that happen on the court and say, 'This is what works, and this is what doesn't work.' If you're going to be hard on yourself for making a mistake—and I made a big one—you have to be able to do it in a constructive way." A routine is there to help you overcome the challenges, large and small, that may interfere with your A-game. As we discussed in Chapter 6 on self-talk, Rennae told me about how self-talk was an important part of her routine. Now let's work to develop your routine.

The Answer Is Within You:
Let Your Success Guide Your Routine

Think back to a moment when you performed well. This could be a particular conversation, meeting, presentation, or sporting event in which you really "killed it." In the box below write down what you felt like. What were the emotions, sensations, or feelings you experienced?

Now think back to the things you did before that moment. Try to focus on the things you did that were practicable and under your control. Focus on actions or thoughts linked directly and causally to feeling at the top of your game and in the moment—for example, the type of music you listened to or the thoughts you were thinking before and during your performance. Try to stay away from superstitious parts of the experience such as what you were wearing unless the physical comfort of the clothes affected your confidence or state of mind. Write a list of the thoughts or behaviors you observed that led to your peak moment.

The next step is to go through your list and add strategies from the anxiety and motivation chapters that you could add to make your routine more robust. You should also go back and add info from the self-talk and visualization chapters. For example, if you noticed that you were more relaxed and feeling loose when you had your successful performance, go ahead and try to add a centering breath before you begin to perform next time. If you noticed that you were having positive thoughts during the performance, try adding more efficiency to the routine by adding a self-talk mantra you can repeat while you are in the moment.

It can also be helpful to have pre-performance, during-performance (resetting), and post-performance routines. After reviewing all the chapters in the book, come back to the worksheet and list up to three steps you will take before competing at life in your big moment and up to three things you can think or do differently to keep yourself locked in and ready to compete!

Pre-performance Routine:
1.
2.
3.

During-performance Routine:
1.
2.
3.

Post-performance Routine:
1.
2.
3.

Keep Experimenting

Baseball great Ken Griffey Jr. hit the ball on the screws when he said, "To succeed in baseball as in life you must make adjustments." For a routine to be truly great, it needs to evolve. Try adding and subtracting to your routine to find what works best for you. Does listening to particular song work better in getting you ready than another? Does a certain stretch work better at centering you? Does getting to a meeting early leave you feeling better, or is your energy better arriving just in time? The more your routines evolve to your present-day challenges and the more you adjust your thoughts and behaviors (the D and T of DOT) to the people, surroundings, and other conditions, the more the best version of you will show up—and win!

Enjoyment Exercise

Take a break from setting up a real routine that you're working on and come up with a routine that feels silly or will make you laugh or one that will bring up good feelings or a positive state of mind. For instance, tell yourself that every time you've been sitting for ten minutes, you get up and dance to a favorite song of yours as a way to not only enjoy the moment but also to practice having a routine that actually encourages you to remember to have a little fun. Challenge yourself to be playful with a colleague, friend, or teammate. I once wore a monkey suit to a daughter's fifth grade classroom on her birthday, and it transformed my relationship with the entire class (in a good way). This one act increased the playfulness in my interactions with those students until they graduated from the school three

years later. Now I revive that routine by wearing the suit or engaging in a similarly ridiculous activity at the school on a regular basis. Try to push your limits by changing your routine to
say hello to a stranger or smile at someone you don't normally
talk to.

Conclusion

Win Today

Success and failure are both part of life, whether you're competing in front of forty-five thousand screaming fans or talking one-on-one to a potential client from your office. In my view success is subjective. At the end of the day (or the game), those who succeed are the people who can look back and know that they were fully present in their lives and worked as hard as they could to be the best version of themselves they could be. This book is a result of a decade of work in sports and performance psychology. Living life as sport—that is, to win by competing with myself to enjoy every minute of the competition—has been a lesson I have learned in the process.

You don't have to look any further to see those lessons played out than on your television during the baseball playoffs every year. In 2015 the New York Mets went on a strong second-half run to win the division, then played inspired baseball to beat the Los Angeles Dodgers three games to two in the divisional series and the Chicago Cubs in the NLCS in a four-game sweep to win the Pennant. After both of those series wins the Mets players basked in what is truly a massive accomplishment, spraying champagne and celebrating the culmination of thousands of hours of preparation, work, and stress.

David Wright, the Mets team captain and third baseman, is emblematic of a player who can live life as sport. His relentless work ethic is matched by his ability to fully enjoy the game to which he has dedicated his life. At the end of the 2015 series David showed his passion to enjoy the process during a year that was in many ways an uphill battle: "When I look back on this year, it will be the best time that I ever had on the baseball field. . . . This truly was special."[1] He went on to later describe what this enjoyment did for his outlook, "The whole experience has me fired up for the 2016 season."

The ability to fully experience and enjoy all parts of the competition, all parts of life, without running from them, is a skill, and one the Mets mastered on their way to winning the pennant in 2015. When you derive enjoyment from the process, you lead a more satisfying *and* successful life. Practicing enjoyment prepares you for battle and helps you overcome obstacles. You too can decide to fully be there, to practice with a passion for growth, to show up in the game of life. And when you do, you always win.

Your Path to Enjoyment and Success

I don't read minds. But my job with any elite athlete—and with you here—is to help you understand your own thoughts and motivations and come up with the right plan to optimize the way you think and act. Now that you've made your way through *Life as Sport*, you have the same set of tools my professional clients use to not only win more championships but also to embrace and enjoy the journey, even if it leads to a second—or seventh—place finish. Because a first-place finish doesn't feel good if you can't enjoy it.

Just like that nagging home improvement project you've been putting off for two months, having the tools at hand is only the first step in creating a solution. In this chapter I'll show you how to use the tools we've been developing over the last seven chapters to implement real changes in your life. Does it mean you won't ever have a tough sales quarter or a bust of an annual meeting or go through the normal scrapes and rough patches everybody experiences? No.

But when I've done my job, my clients are better equipped to handle adversity when it comes, both in terms of managing their emotions and behavior as they go through, and keeping it in the proper perspective.

They both win better and lose better.

The most successful professional relationships I have with athletes and elite performers in other disciplines are those where we're able to work out a long-range plan. And my goal with *Life as Sport* is to have that experience with you. I don't want this book to end up collecting dust on your shelf—an unfortunate fate that awaits many of the books in this "self-improvement" genre.

I don't mean to imply that other books don't provide solid information and can't help you—they can. But the best guides are the ones that offer a capstone action plan to synthesize all that's come before.

That is this chapter.

This is your purposeful practice plan.

Purposeful Practice

What does that mean?

I've been at hundreds of baseball games hours before the first pitch, watching hitters take batting practice in a nearly empty stadium. It is easy to tell when hitters are just going through the motions, half paying attention to what is going on. Maybe they're thinking about where they want to eat after the game or whether the good-looking woman from the night before is going to be in the stands later. Or maybe they're grinding away on some mechanical tip from the hitting coach or seething over a slump or a sharp comment about them on *SportsCenter* the night before.

That kind of thing isn't confined to elite athletes. How many times have you gotten in your car or on a train or bus on your way to work and drifted off into half-attention, only to arrive at work with no real memory of the trip? Or zone out as you watch your kids playing at the playground, returning to awareness only as you hear the notification chime for Facebook or Twitter on your phone?

Real practice is different.

Fully committing yourself to your improvement routine requires much more energy and application of will than many people are used to expending. That's why it's called *purposeful practice*—something you're doing very intentionally.

In more than a decade of coaching elite performers, I've seen what it takes to commit to purposeful practice. I liken this type of practice to turning up the brightness on your cell phone display. When we fully commit to practice and give our attention to living life as sport, everything is brighter, crisper, and more colorful. It isn't enough to read through the chapters in this—or any—book and make a plan or to tell yourself that you "want it." The real energy and boost required for purposeful practice has to come from the two concepts that have been central to this book: motivation and enjoyment (ME).

As we discussed in the chapter on motivation, it's very hard to be good at the "what" and "how" in life if you haven't solidly identified the "*why*" for completing your goals. Knowing your deep motivation, or Power Value, for peak performance is essential in actually bringing out the best of what's inside you. When you think of your Power Value or Values, what exactly is your motivation to continue living your life as a sport and truly incorporating the strategies in this book into how you live day-to-day? Why do you want to make every day a game day and bring out your very best in your relationship or work? Go ahead and write a few sentences about your reasons for committing to this journey:

What are your thoughts upon reading your motivation to continue to practice? How can you be more specific to get at the heart of why you want to make the concepts and strategies in this book an integral part of your life? Why do you want to prevent the book and its ideas from gathering literal and metaphorical dust? The more specific you can get, the more likely you are to be able to put yourself in that purposeful practice zone over and over again. Review your core Power Values from Chapter 3. How does this Power Value connect to your goals? Post your Power Value and your reasons for purposeful practice in a place where you will be reminded of your motivation. Make reminding yourself of your motivations a part of your routine. By practicing internalizing an awareness of these motivations, you are adding more potent fuel to your tank that will help you sustain your drive to practice, even when the going gets tough.

Of course, plenty of top athletes are supremely motivated. Is that enough?

It can be. But if all you have is motivation, the wins can be much more hollow. After all, what is winning if you can't enjoy it? True satisfaction comes from relishing the opportunity to compete and to play, to find enjoyment in the process more than the outcome.

We've spent a lot of time talking about how to incorporate the practice of enjoyment into your self-talk, routines, goal setting, and visualization, which hopefully means you're learning how to think and act in ways that promote more enjoyment, not just raw "wins" or "losses." When we were kids we were naturally programmed to enjoy our performance. As we mature, the pressures of achievement can take away our ability to simply be present in our joy of competing. The exercises in each chapter are meant to

help you stay in the moment by reconnecting to the simple plea-
sures of performing and competing in what you do.

Laird Hamilton said it well when he described to me this
sense of connection. "It's why I live the way I do," he said. "You
have a better life when you make your life like a sport. Your jobs
are better. Your moods are better. Your successes are greater. You
enhance your life by treating it as if it's a performance. I have a
friend who is a professional athlete, and I told him, 'You go into
a stadium and you've got fifty thousand people cheering your
name or booing you. To contrast that, you have to go in the
middle of the desert where nobody is and hang out by a rock or
under a tree just to create balance in your life. Don't get into a
fantasy world or delusion, where the stadium is the most important thing to you. You need to create balance and find your
equilibrium.'" In this view, living life as sport is finding the balance to work on being your best self while you practice enjoying
the moment.

Regardless of the objective score in your particular game—
on the Jumbotron at the baseball stadium or in the sales ranking
at your company—if you are really working to *do* things that
help you enjoy a meeting more (e.g., complimenting colleagues,
sitting in a way that makes you comfortable, etc.) and you are
thinking in a way that increases enjoyment (e.g., asking yourself
what you enjoyed most, thinking about what you found most
beautiful or humorous about a meeting or other interaction)
you're bound to have a more satisfying experience, which will
likely lead to more success as it is conventionally defined.

Why?

Because you will be performing in a more relaxed, more positive state, which takes less mental stress and toll and allows you
to operate at a higher functional level for longer.

The daily ritual of baseball batting practice I mentioned above is a perfect example. Some players privately grumble about the day-to-day grind of batting practice because they believe it's almost impossible to stay "locked in" for thirty minutes of the same potentially monotonous activity over and over again for six months in a row.

But the player who works to find something enjoyable about the process of batting practice will be much more likely to stay connected to what is happening for the full thirty minutes, day after day, and will get the full benefit of seeing all those pitches and making all those swings. The players I observe laughing with teammates about an awkward swing, making a game about who can hit more homers, and just chatting in between batting groups are usually the ones who perform better over the long haul.

In my line of work we certainly love performance benefits, but that isn't even the biggest bonus that comes with truly embracing the concept of enjoying the process. What focusing on enjoying the process really does is free you from some of the performance pressure that is so pervasive in virtually every business—along with the undeserved stigma of failure.

I use the term "undeserved" very specifically because I want to differentiate between failure that comes as a natural part of taking risks and failure that comes from being unprepared, unmotivated, or unorganized. When you use your tools to the best of your ability, embrace the process, and enjoy the journey, you haven't failed—no matter what the scoreboard says. You did what you could do, you saw the sights and interacted with interesting people, and you picked up some valuable lessons for the next journey.

That's a win.

Bobby Cannavale, star of *Vinyl* and *Boardwalk Empire*, told me a great story about how he measures himself within his profession. "Nobody is going to keep giving me work just because I've won awards or because I'm a nice guy. They have to believe I can do it, and I have to believe I can do it," says Cannavale. "So I go into each opportunity and do my research so I can be enthusiastic about it and figure out how I can connect with the character and get on board with him. To use a baseball term, I'm on my front foot, so to speak. Working on being as confident and motivated as possible in general is like batting practice for life. And after I put in my work in rehearsals, I have full confidence that I'm the master of it. The validation of getting hired—getting the chance to say, 'Wow, they want me to play something,' and having diverse characters to play and different opportunities, that's what keeps me going."

Compare Cannavale's description of his process to the too-common stories you hear about relentless sports and business competitors who never seem to register any satisfaction with what they've experienced or achieved.

They may be dominating professional golf, tennis, or football, but after injuries and age creep in, they aren't dominating as they once did. Their day-to-day performance looks like physical and mental torture. In these athletes you don't see the baseline love of the game that is so evident in many of sport's greatest performers. When they are sitting with their grandkids at age seventy, talking about those great years, will they be proud of what they accomplished or disappointed that they didn't accomplish more? Moreover, what will *you* be saying to your grandchildren? It's a question I ask all professional athletes to help them reflect on the practice of enjoyment. When you hang up your cleats, how do you want to be remembered? How do you want to remember your playing years? The same question can help to orient you in your action plan for living your life as sport. When you retire, how do *you* want to be remembered? How do *you* want to feel when you look back on the years when you were truly striving to be the best professional, parent, or spouse you could be? Your answer may direct you toward practicing enjoying things more and working toward using the techniques and suggestions in this book to be more present in every moment as you try to be your best self in the game of life.

To preserve the playfulness and joy that should come as a part of *Life as Sport*, think back on the strategies and individual performer anecdotes we talked about over the last seven chapters. Which ones were the most enjoyable to read? Where could you see connections to parts of yourself and your own journey? What are the specific reasons you connected that way, and what can you take as your own tool?

Taking Action

Speeches and plans are great, but peak performers take one critical step that connects their intention and attitude with reality and results.

They put in the reps.

Now it's time to make the whole of *Life as Sport* an integrated part of your life routine. Let's take another look at the pillars of the *Life as Sport* philosophy and the techniques you have learned while reading this book.

GOAL SETTING
MOTIVATIONAL ENHANCEMENT
MANAGING ANXIETY
VISUALIZATION
SELF-TALK
ROUTINES

ENJOYMENT

OBJECTIVE OPTIMISM

PRESENT AND FUTURE ORIENTATION

PROCESS FOCUS

© Jonathan Fader • www.jonathanfader.com

How can you incorporate the philosophy and techniques of *Life as Sport* into your daily life? Go back to our discussion about the DOT model in Chapter 2.

What can you *do* and what can you *think* to get the *outcome* you want? In this case, the desired result is to integrate this book and its philosophies and techniques into your life! Below you will find the DOT model once again so you can write in what you plan to *do* and how you plan to *think* right next to each letter to help you to retain your progress attributed to reading this book.

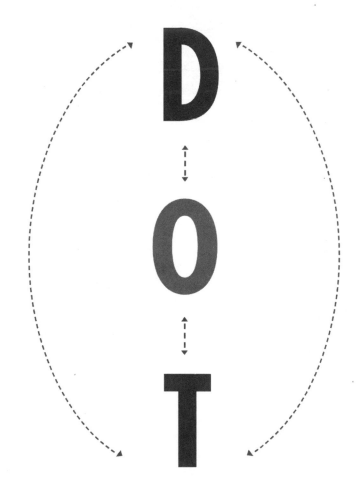

Here are some things you might write in the *Doing* section:

- Implement a *Life as Sport* routine into your wake-up, before-work, or before-bed activities
- Make a list of the specific strategies: self-talk, visualization, anxiety management, building motivation, goal setting, and routines. Which of these techniques spoke to you the most? Which chapters made you the most hopeful about improving your performance?
- Pick out a few of those techniques and determine how they will fit into your daily schedule.
- Start a discussion group or book club with others interested in the *Life as Sport* concepts.
- Keep a journal of your progress.
- Have a routine to remind you of your motivation to achieve your goal.
- Have an enjoyment routine, such as a daily question, meditation, or conversation with a specific person to remind yourself to focus and experience what you enjoy about your competitive environment.
- Write a post on how you are living your life as a sport on social media, sharing your observations on your motivations/enjoyment on Facebook or in a private online forum.
- Call a friend to update them on your progress.
- Reread the book (or chapters) at some regular interval.
- Take notes on the book and review.
- Listen to the book online to ensure the concepts and techniques are well encoded.
- Visit the *Life as Sport* website to practice with the interactive material there.
- Share the book's ideas with those around you at parties, events, and other gatherings.

Here are some things you might write in the *Thinking* section:

- Ask yourself daily, "What do I enjoy about applying the *Life as Sport* philosophy?"
- Ask yourself daily, "What is my motivation to use *Life as Sport* strategies to improve my life?"
- Figure out your main obstacles to forgetting the lessons you learned and think about how you will overcome them.
- Mentally review the objectively optimistic thought process that will lead you to feel the most confident in your work or relationship.
- Fine-tune your mantra to a few powerful words.
- Think out several mantras that help you in different situations or performance states.
- Think up an "enjoyment" mantra, such as "Be here" or "This moment."
- Ask yourself, "What is a mantra that will help me stay on track in my purposeful practice?"
- Develop a mobilizing mantra to improve your acceptance of your procrastination, inconsistency, or inefficiency, such as "I will do my best and my best is all I can do" or "I accept my setbacks and will now move on."
- Be gentle and forgiving of yourself in accepting your thoughts.

Now you can go back and write down a few actions and thoughts or reactions that you can put in place to create an action plan that will increase your chances of achieving an optimal outcome.

Like any long-range behavior-changing plan, such as weight loss or learning a new language from scratch, you need to be committed to the change and accountable for what you do and don't do. Try to come up with at least one Doing (behaving) goal and one Thinking goal that you can work on for your purposeful practice. If you fall off for a day or a week, that's okay! What's most important is that you work to get back on track as soon as possible! Don't fall victim to the abstinence violation effect (Chapter 2)! You can start again on any purposeful practice plan, and any practice, no matter how small, of the *Life as Sport* techniques or philosophy should help you enjoy your life more and contribute to improved results.

Success Story

One of my favorite success stories from the *Life as Sport* model doesn't come from a high-profile athlete I've worked with or one my Wall Street traders or performing artists; it comes from a salesman named Sam. After having had a successful sales career, Sam had hit a wall in his late forties. He wasn't as productive as he had been previously. He had heard about my work in professional sports and how I used similar perspectives and techniques to help people in all walks of life perform at their best. When he walked into my office he was shocked.

"What is that!?" he asked immediately, pointing to my conference table that turns into a ping-pong table. He was equally stunned by my stand-up desk with a treadmill underneath. I explained to him that it was my belief that enjoyment was a skill to be practiced, that I had only a certain number of minutes to live, and if I was going to be typing or having meetings, I wanted to make damn sure that I was enjoying those activities to the absolute maximum.

Stunned, Sam looked at me with a half-smile. "You're not like the other shrinks I've seen," he said.

"No. In fact, I prefer to think of myself as a *stretch*, not a shrink," I said.

He was enthused that I view my job as building on people's strengths and not just focusing on what's wrong. I've learned that from the best coaches in the major leagues. Always focus on what the player *should do*, not what they shouldn't do.

Sam and I discussed his goals. He wanted to make more money and to improve his relationships with his kids. We had some work to do to redesign his goals to be more process oriented (see Chapter 2 on goal setting). We needed to think of the actions and thoughts that, if practiced, would lead to in improvement in those outcomes. In other words, I helped him to focus on the D and T of DOT. He and I established that we would focus on improving the quality of his sales calls and his follow-up as well. In addition, he decided he would be working on creating and maintaining better communication with his children.

When I asked him why he wanted to achieve these things, he shrugged at first. "I don't know, I just know I need to," he said.

You know me well enough by now to know that I don't go for that! I pushed on and found deeper Power Values behind his desire to achieve eventual success in these areas. When I asked him what was at stake if he didn't reach these goals, I saw his eyes glisten and he nearly whispered, "I want my kids to have a chance to really be the best they can be. I feel that I only achieved a fraction of my potential, and I know if I can be more successful, I will show them that it is possible. The money I will make is also a means to send them to the type of schools that will help to ensure their success."

After elaborating in the way he did, Sam sat up straighter. It was as though he had more resolve and focus to develop the routines, self-talk, and visualization he would need to assist him in performing optimally on his calls. We developed a simple and elegant routine for him. In the morning he would get up, and the first thing he would do is remind himself of his Power Values: self-esteem, responsibility, and purpose. Building on our work together, he had shared his values with his wife and children, and his son, a graphic artist, had set these words in a hip font for him to tape to his mirror. Every morning he gassed up by looking at these words and reminding himself that the reason he wanted to fully live his life as sport was to improve his self-esteem so he could model for his kids how to value themselves. He was made more aware of his sense of responsibility to them and how they led him to feel more purposeful in his daily sales endeavors. From there Sam would take a shower, but instead of just letting the water hit him and zone out in a completely nonpurposeful way, he would spend the five minutes in the shower visualizing his day. He would see himself smiling at coworkers, joking confidently on the phone, and positively responding to adversity. He also practiced accepting any less-than-ideal outcomes for feelings and moving on by using his several practiced self-talk mantras that would be available to him during the day, including "Be in the moment," "Every 'no' brings me closer to a 'yes,'" "I can always find enjoyment," and "Just this phone call."

At work Sam had a great ritual that he invented as a result of our discussions. If he had a micro-failure, if something small didn't go his way on a sales call, he immediately got up and did something physical, like push-ups, jumping jacks, or stretching. This was effective from a resetting perspective and also had the unexpected effect of making Sam somewhat of an office celebrity, as all of his coworkers thought he was hilarious! When he found himself overwhelmed on a day with poor outcome or when the other things we were working on didn't seem to do the trick, he simply focused on his breathing—four seconds in, four seconds out, one- to two-second pause—until he was able to get back to the other skills we practiced. This breathing helped him center himself and "empty his mind."

Each time we met, Sam and I reviewed his ME (motivation and enjoyment). He practiced his motivation by reiterating why he was doing all this hard work, and we discussed the aspects of his struggle for self-improvement that he enjoyed. In time he found that there were even some aspects of his hard work that, when he stopped fighting them, became enjoyable. For example, he used to dread performance reviews. He found his boss to be critical and thought the whole semi-annual critique was too staged and not individualized. As we worked together, Sam and I began to help him redirect his self-criticism into a more objectively optimistic viewpoint. However critical his supervisor was, Sam worked to ask himself, "Where is the treasure here?" Once he was able to accept his boss's critical voice and distance himself a bit, he could then take a different perspective. He was shocked when he could actually find small truths ("treasures") in his boss's general and somewhat insensitive observations. He was further stunned when this change in outlook brought some enjoyment. He began to look forward to telling me how, like an alchemist, he had changed the "inane" things his boss had said into gems of self-knowledge.

Every time we met I asked Sam about what he enjoyed most about the time he spent with his kids. He kept a journal in his phone and had a daily goal of writing about one minute during the day in which he experienced enjoyment with his son or his two daughters. He tended to write one thing a day that he felt thankful for about their relationship or spending time with them. He found that when he practiced this, it led to a different perspective on all the other minutes in which he found himself struggling or otherwise momentarily unsuccessful. I'm telling you this story not only because it illustrates how many of the techniques and ideas of this book can synthesize for someone who is not an elite athlete but also because it had a profound effect on me. Sam wasn't always successful in our work. Overall his relationship with his kids got even better and he made more money. I have certainly worked with many traders who made many millions during our work together. But with Sam there were ups and downs. However, what stands out to me is how good he got at enjoying competing in his life. He relished each call like a major league at-bat. Each day with his kids turned into a playoff game. Sam will always stick with me because of how hard he played life as sport. I found that whatever the outcomes were, I really enjoyed working with him.

Trying Something New

I'm the definition of a city kid. I was raised in Manhattan, and I've lived the majority of my life in either Manhattan or Brooklyn. So when I take a trip down South, as I have many times to visit minor league baseball parks, I sometimes feel like I'm visiting a strange land. It has the same language as home, but the patterns are different. It's slower and hotter, but in a way I have learned to love.

One trip down South was more special than any of the others.

I drove the winding back roads outside Asheville, North Carolina, to pay a visit to one of the true legends in the field of elite performance and baseball psychology, a guy named Harvey Dorfman.

A journalist by trade, Harvey came to baseball by a circuitous route, working with various teams and eventually winning World Series rings with the Oakland A's and Florida Marlins for his work as the team mental coach.

Harvey had agreed to meet and share some insight on what had made him so successful and what he was doing to continue to expand the reach of mental-skills training as a consultant for agent Scott Boras's organization.

I felt lucky to get the time with Harvey. After all, he was the guy who had coined the term I sometimes use for the work I do in performance: *stretch*. Harvey warned me in a letter that he wasn't well (indeed, he passed away not too long after our visit, in 2011) and that he might not be able to spend much time with me. But I was hopeful as I drove up to his beautiful house, and his lovely wife, Anita, greeted me with some of North Carolina's finest brownies.

We settled into Harvey's office, surrounded by a career's worth of museum-quality artifacts—signed gloves, bats, and balls—and Harvey opened our conversation in his characteristic way: "Tell me your story."

I described for him my background and how exciting it was helping athletes make the jump into the highest level of performance—and how challenging it was that so many players in the business of sports didn't yet value how important mental skills training is.

Harvey responded by sharing his story, and it was filled with colorful scenes that could have been in every baseball movie ever filmed. From his time with the A's to working with future Hall-of-Famers like Roy Halladay, he described some truly inspiring experiences. He also brought the coaching of elite performers back to the common threads that connect every human. "They bleed just like you and I do," he said. "They just do it in public."

But one thing Harvey said stood out more than anything else. "Scared money don't make no money," he said. "You gotta have courage, kid."

Plenty of advice Harvey gave me that day kept me involved in professional sports. In turn I was able to have the experiences that led to the philosophies you've read about in this book, but that single concept—the *willingness* to take risks and put yourself out there for success—is so important to share here, at the end of our journey.

"By avoiding asking the hard question or being too scared to try the new idea you have, you avoid getting yelled at or failing, but you'll never be great," Harvey said. "Greatness only comes to those who try something new, who go out on a limb and shake up the system."

We talked for hours, until the sun went down, and I shook hands with my new friend. I took his advice with me, and it's one thing I want to leave here with you.

After working your way through this book you have the tools. You have a plan. You have the ideas, strategies, and concepts you need to shake up your own life and take some new risks, both big and small.

Now it's up to you.

You can put this book back on the shelf or leave it in the pocket on the back of the airline seat in front of you. You can delete it from your Kindle or give it to your nephew for his ride back home. Or you can keep it and treat it like an owner's manual for your competitive mind. Pick one of the concepts we discuss in any chapter and commit to the process of getting comfortable with being uncomfortable. Change is hard, and it *will* feel strange.

But I'll tell you the same thing I tell every client who sits with me in my office on Union Square in Manhattan: *you're the expert on you.* I won't pretend to know better than you do your life or what will work for you. But I do know what tools work for the journey and how to set you up for that trip. It's often not the change itself that people resist; it's the hard work of the transition and that first leap of faith. The fact that you got through the book and committed to fully learn this approach gives me faith that you will be able to engage in a purposeful practice plan that will impact your life.

Even with all the commercials, a World Series or Super Bowl game usually lasts less than four hours. It goes by fast for the players on the field. Life lasts longer, but it goes by at the same shocking speed. And life is every bit of the performance a baseball or football game is.

Now it's your time, and it's ticking by quickly. You have your own at-bat, race, or match in the form of a conversation, meeting, presentation, or sales call. How courageous will you be at challenging your limits? How good can you get at embracing—and enjoying—the battle to be your very best?

The national anthem has been sung.
They played your theme music.
The crowd is going wild.
Now it's time to face that first pitch.

Enjoyment Exercise

Every night before I went to bed as a kid my mom would ask me what I was most grateful for. I was allowed five things—but no repeats! Today I do a similar exercise with my kids, but I add in the question, "What did you enjoy most about the day?" Now ask yourself, "What did you enjoy most about reading this book? What is it about the idea of living your life as a sport—as an elite athlete competes in their arena—that has moved you, inspired you, or led you to believe you can gain more success or satisfaction?" Write a sentence or two that distills what you most enjoyed. By being grateful for what you have and enjoying each performance, you will not only be your best; you will truly be living your life as a sport in every moment.

GRATITUDE

A big debt a gratitude to goes to Gillian Mackenzie, my super-agent. You are living proof that having the best coach is hugely helpful in truly living life as a sport. From the moment of this book's conception, to the writing of these acknowledgments, you have been a thoughtful advisor. You believed in me and in this book, and there is no replacement for that kind of support and encouragement. Thank you. (Also, thanks to Kirsten Wolf and Allison Devereux for all your hard work behind the scenes).

I feel privileged to have had the support of my editor at Da Capo. Dan Ambrosio, you are a pro's pro. From the get-go, you understood this book and my vision, working to make sure that it would fulfill its true potential editorially and conceptually—so much so that I'll forgive your team allegiance! Thanks, man! There are many folks at Da Capo who helped bring this project to fruition. Many thanks also to Miriam Riad for your tireless organization. Thanks to Lori Hobkirk and Josephine Moore for attending to each and every detail in project management and copyediting—you are the epitome of efficiency and patience. Thanks to Lissa Warren, Michael Giarratano, and Kevin Hanover for helping to get this book everywhere it is meant to go! You are all part of Life As Sport!

Matt Rudy: huge thanks to you for all your work in revising, editing, and researching this book. You helped me make this book even better! Thanks for all your tireless work in attending to all the details! And thanks for taking the journey with me across these eighteen holes!

Katie "KINGZ" Krimer: Wow! You deserve cappuccinos for life. Thanks for editing, reading, harassing, purchasing, researching, reminding, harassing again, following up, taking care of business, thinking about stuff, imagining, brainstorming, and harassing again. You are a tremendous coordinator and friend to me and to this book!!! FACE. FACE. FACE.

Alec "OPPS" Opperman: Dang, man. Let's hope this story ends with a windowed office. Thanks for lending all your creativity and time to spend with me in the world of ideas. From discussing the fine points of visualization to supervising all the talented interns who work at Union Square Practice, you really improved the overall quality of this book! I sincerely hope you never escape Union Square Practice.

Keira "Wonder Woman" Rakoff: Maybe I should write one last chapter in this book about you. I'd call it "DEDICATION." Thanks for keeping things on track for me so that I could find the time to write this!

Taylor Grant: Thank you for your illustration and design talents. You definitely focus on the D and T for a great OUTCOME. Can't wait to collaborate with you on the next illustration project!

Dr. Michael Dulchin: You've been many things to me in my life to date—mentor, friend, business partner. Regarding this book, you have been a wise voice, colleague, and nurturer. Thanks for your support and for taking the helm of Union Square Practice when I couldn't take my shift. I feel lucky to have built such a vibrant place to work and help people, and I can't imagine doing it with anyone else.

Ron Gonen: Thanks for all your thoughtfulness and advice during the writing process. You are a champion of this book and the most solid of friends. . . . Scratch that—brothers. THANK YOU!

Dr. Jeff Foote: From the moment I walked into Smither's (I wasn't wearing ripped jeans!) to the writing of our early work together in baseball, you have shown me the way to enjoy so many opportunities, sometimes because you just pushed me in the door, but mostly because you are someone who embraces stress as a challenge and not a threat, and you are a person who values personal connection and relationships above all else. If it weren't for you, I wouldn't be walking the path I'm on now. Thanks for carrying the torch and for blazing some serious trails! Thanks for valuing our relationship and for supporting me.

Sandy Alderson: Thank you for your support, encouragement, guidance, honesty, humor, and above all else, thanks for your example of what it is to be an exemplary human.

I am very grateful to the New York Mets for giving me the opportunity and support to work in one of the greatest sport organizations in the world. The lessons I have learned from working with the players, coaches, and front office folks have been greater than I could ever learn in any class. In particular, I would like to note the tremendous leadership of Sandy Alderson, John Ricco, Paul DePodesta, and JP Riccardi. You guys have motivated me to be at my best. In addition, none of my work could have been accomplished without the vision and support of Fred and Jeff Wilpon and Saul Katz: thank you. The cast of characters at the Mets is very long, but everyone in the organization has been important to me in one way or another. I want to thank Terry Collins for his support for my work in the minor and major leagues over six inspiring years. I would also like to thank Ricky Bones, Bob Geren, Tom Goodwin, Dave Hudgens, Kevin Long, Pat Roessler, Tim Teufel, Dan Warthen, Lamar Johnson, Luis Natera, Guy Conti, Dave Racaniello, and Eric Langill. Big thanks to Dick Scott, Kevin Morgan, Bob Natal, Rick Waits, Ron Romanick, Jon Debus, Wally Backman, Frank Viola, Jack Voight, Benny Distefano, Pedro Lopez, Glenn Abott, Luis Rojas, Phil Regan, Joel Fuentes, Jose Leger, Marc Valdes, Ryan Ellis, Tom Gamboa, Tom Signore, Yunir Garcia, George Greer, Hector Berrios, Luis Rivera, Jonathan Hurst, Jose Carreno, Rafael Landestoy, and Ryan Ellis. I learned an incredible amount from dozens of other managers, coaches, trainers, and strength and conditioning staff I have worked with for more than six years in the minor leagues who reinforced what I always knew—that it's all about the relationship. Your care for the players as humans first and players second continues to inspire me to this day.

Special Thanks to Dr. Derick Anderson and Ruben Aybar for being my partners in mental skills training. D, I'm looking forward to many more pickle-free lunches during which we continue to learn from each other. Thanks for all your advice and thoughtfulness over the past few years. You have been my sounding board and wise man for three years now . . . let's make it thirty!

Big thanks to the best trainers in baseball: Ray Ramirez, Brian Chicklo, Mark Rogow, Mike Herbst, Joe Golia, Deb Iwanow, Matt Hunter, Eric Velasquez, and Kiyoshi Tada!

Big thanks to John Zajac, Jason "Nitro" Craig, Dustin Clarke, Mike Barwis, Brian Small, Kevin Keirst, Dave Berni, Jim Malone, Dave Pearson, Theresa Corderi, and Ma!

I'd also like to thank the other Mets folks who have worked with me over the years: David Newman, David Cohen, Holly "SH" Lindvall, June Napoli, Harold Kaufman, Adam Fisher, Tommy Tanous, Ian Levin, TJ Barra, Bryan Hayes, Jim Kelly, Jay Horowitz, Jon Miller, Bryn Alderson, Ronny Reyes, Donovan Mitchell, Rob Kasdon, Kathy Fullam, Jennifer Wolf, Michelle Holmes, Adam Wogan, and Rafael Perez.

Thanks to my Grandfather, Colonel Bernard Koch, DVM. I hope you are reading this where you are . . . in one way or another, you are in this book.

Thanks to the staff and colleagues of the American Psychological Association, Association for Behavioral and Cognitive Therapies, the Association for Applied Sport Psychology, and the Motivational Interviewing Network of Trainers. Participation and membership in these excellent professional groups over the last fifteen years has deepened my appreciation for empirically supported sport and performance psychology, Cognitive Behavioral Therapy, and Motivational Interviewing. This training background is the cornerstone that prepared me to help people change their lives and to write this book.

Thanks to all the folks at the MLB Players Association: Dr. Joel Solomon, Dr. John Mariani, Tony Clark, Dave Winfield, Steve Rogers, Omar Minaya, Rick Helling, Jose Cruz Jr., Jeffrey Hammonds, Steve Rogers, Bob Lenaghan, Dave Prouty, Leonor Barua, Allyne Price, and Gene Orza.

Thanks to Dr. Larry Westrich and John Coyles, Brian O'Gara, Yenifer Fauche, and Jerimah Yolkut at MLB.

Thanks to my mentors: doctors Mary Larimer, Alan Marlatt, Jeff Foote, Red Schiller, Goldie Alfasi, Susan Sussman, Mike Quitman, Bob Feldman, Jason Kilmer, Joel Solomon, and

Ron Smith. You have all shown me—on a personal level—what "self-efficacy" is all about. Thank you. Thank you. Thank you.

Union Square Practice: Thank you for all your genuine feedback about this book and for making our workplace such an exciting place to be! I'm lucky to be surrounded by such talented and warm individuals who are okay with me pranking them from time to time:

Alec Opperman, Ashley Mason, Dr. Dana Rhule, Danielle Conklin, Dr. Jamye Shelton Pelosi, Dr. Jessica Stack, Dr. Julia Vigna Bosson, Dr. Kate Thacher, Katie Krimer, Keira Rakoff, Dr. Laura Paret, Matt Buttigieg, Michelle Freedland, and Dr. Mike Dulchin.

Thanks to all the Union Square Practice interns of past, present, and future: Kristina Flemming, Michaela Green, Simone Cooper, Leanne Gueits, Jeremy Rahn, Marielle Goebelbecker, Jia Gao, Lianna Trubowitz, and Kenneth Cavanagh

Thanks to Drs. Denise Festa, Angus Mugford, Ken Ravizza, and Judson Miller for reviewing the earlier drafts. Big shout out to Angus for the Pillars illustration idea!

Big thanks to the talented Katherine Schulten for her editorial artistry and for supporting all my Willy Wonka ways.

Gracias, Justin Su'a. "Started on Twitter, now we're here!"

Shout outs to the whole Howard Family, especially Jenine!

Thanks, Gabby Reece and big thanks to Jenn Meredith for going beyond the call of duty.

Thanks to all those who put me in touch with great people: Emilio Collins, Lisa Smith-Greenberg, and Ron Gonen (again!).

Thanks to the best clubhouse eva! Ruomi Lee-Hampel, Chinyelu Ingram, Danny Greenberg, Tim Wersan, Chris Temme, Ron Gonen (again), and Nikolai Moderbocher.

Thanks Dr. Drew Ramsey, Dr. Ben Michaelis, and Jared Tendler for all your book encouragement!

Thanks Jason Brezler for keeping Brooklyn safe and for your support and interest in my work.

Thanks to Amogh Havanur for his early work in assisting with the book proposal.

Big thanks to Dr. Ray Karesky,

Thanks and more thanks to: all the west coast Koch/Candelarias! Doug, Lauren, Linda, and George Weiss. Tsuya Yee, Dr. David Koch, Jeffrey Karaban, Dave Valle, Katherine Schulten, Dr. Bukky Kolowale, Pyeng Threadgill, Paul Gaiger, John Siffert, Howard Crystal, Dr. Kate Porterfield, Dr. Ben Brennan, and all the Ludgate/Liranzos. Thanks, Dr. Cheryl Rogow, Dr. Annalisa Erba, Steve Kettmann, Dr. Ilana Braun, Dr. Derek Tate, Dr. Jennifer Hartstein, Dr. Alexandra Bloom, Alexa Allen, Sandra Lackovic, Bryan Greene, Dr. James McPartland, Dr. Shireen Rizvi, Julia Rosenthal, Victoria Druziako, Tesa Forsythe, Dr. Michal Seligman, Dr. Leslie Adelstein, Sarah Fader, Gussie Falleder, Jared McShall, Matt Krug, Pedro Pascal, and RON GONEN!

Big thanks to all the members of the Professional Baseball Performance Psychology Group (PBPPG): especially Charlie, Ken, Chad, Geoff, Tewks, Bernie, Don, and Matt for their leadership. I'm proud to be a member of our group. I have learned a lot from all of you and look forward to continuing to learn more.

AJ LaLonde, Andy McKay, Angus Mugford, Bernie Holliday, Bill Springman, Bob Tewksbury, Brian Miles, Brian Peterson, Carrie Stewart, Ceci Clark, Chad Bohling, Charlie Maher, Chris Passarella, Derick Anderson, Derin McMains,

Don Kalkstein, Geoff Miller, Greg Riddoch, Hector Morales-Negron, Jeff Foote, John Fidanza, Josh Lifrak, Josiah Igono, Justin Su'a, Ken Ravizza, Lance Green, Laz Gutierrez, Marc Strickland, Matt Krug, Michael Gerson, Oscar Gutierrez, Richard Ginsburg, Seth Kaplan, Tyson Holt, and Will Lenzner.

Thanks to the contributors: Adrian Grenier, Alvin Williams, Bobby Cannavale, David Winfield, Dr. Eric Potterat, Jason Brezler, John Amaechi, Juwan Howard, Laird Hamilton, Mike Richter, Mike Robinson, Rennae Stubbs, Sam Kass, Sandy Alderson, and Yuri Foreman. I am grateful for your incredible insights and for allowing the readers of this book to get a glimpse of how you live your lives as sport. Your contributions were inspiring!

And, most of all, thanks to the hundreds of players and other elite performers I've known over the years. You have helped me understand—on the most real level—what it means to live life as sport!

Game On!

APPENDIX:

On the following pages you will find additional copies of the Mastery Map and Power Value Motivational Card sort.

You can use these documents for additional practice of the strategies in the goal setting chapter and the chapter on building and sustaining motivation. Also included is a version of the DOT diagram, which can be displayed in your office, locker, or home, as a reminder to yourself of your goal to remain process-focused and to continue to live life as sport.

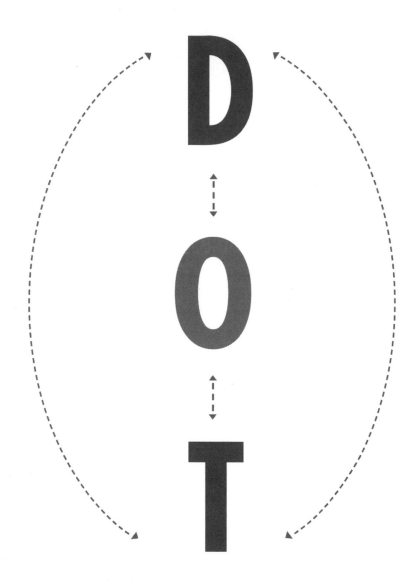

VISUALIZATION
BREATH TRAINING
ROUTINE

DOING

OUTCOME

SELF-TALK, GOAL SETTING, MOTIVATION

FINISH

THINKING

HEALTH

RELATIONSHIPS

ACHIEVEMENT

SELF-ESTEEM

POWER

INDEPENDENCE

PLEASURE

PASSION

WHAT IS YOUR POWER VALUE? DISCOVERING YOUR MOTIVATION

RESPONSIBILITY

COMPASSION

CREATIVITY

LOVE

PURPOSE

GENEROSITY

FAITH

STABILITY

MASTERY MAP

★ YOUR GOAL! ★

HOW WILL YOU MEASURE SUCCESS?

WHO WILL SUPPORT YOU?

FIND YOUR **ENJOYMENT**

CHALLENGES?

HOW WILL YOU GET THERE?

WHAT IS YOUR PROCESS GOAL?

WHAT IS YOUR MOTIVATION? WHAT IS YOUR POWER VALUE?

★ WHAT IS YOUR OUTCOME GOAL? ★

© Jonathan Fader

MASTERY MAP

★ YOUR GOAL! ★

HOW WILL YOU MEASURE SUCCESS?
Refocus my measurements away from my batting average and onto number of pitches seen; hard hit balls; subjective evaluation of my at bat quality (0-100%).

FIND YOUR ENJOYMENT

WHO WILL SUPPORT YOU?
Discussing with my girlfriend, my coach, weekly conversation regarding quality at bats with my coach, talking to my girlfriend about how I've dealt with unwanted results.

CHALLENGES?
A slump; will overcome by reviewing this sheet and discussing with coach.

HOW WILL YOU GET THERE?
Improving my breathing in the batter's box; being diligent about my pre-performance routine (timing pitches while I'm on the on-deck circle) and visualizing; replacing negative self-talk with positive self-talk when encountering unwanted result.

WHAT IS YOUR PROCESS GOAL?
To increase the percentage of quality at bats (seeing more pitches, making more contact, swinging at more good pitches).

WHAT IS YOUR MOTIVATION? WHAT IS YOUR POWER VALUE?
To fulfill my true potential for achievement to set an example of perseverance for younger players.

★ **WHAT IS YOUR OUTCOME GOAL?** ★
Higher batting average.

© Jonathan Fader

MASTERY MAP

★ YOUR GOAL! ★

HOW WILL YOU MEASURE SUCCESS?
Consistency in routines,
subjective quality of the routines.

FIND YOUR ENJOYMENT

WHO WILL SUPPORT YOU?
Coworker on my team.

CHALLENGES?
Tough client questions; distracted clients; physical anxiety
during presentation; USE ADAPTIVE SELF-TALK.

HOW WILL YOU GET THERE?
Visualizing peak performance; centering breath (See chapters 4 & 5).

WHAT IS YOUR PROCESS GOAL?
Maintain calm, confident demeanor before, during, and after presentation.

WHAT IS YOUR MOTIVATION? WHAT IS YOUR POWER VALUE?
Making my mark on the industry—Achievement/Power.

★ **WHAT IS YOUR OUTCOME GOAL?** ★
Make a successful presentation to a potential client.

© Jonathan Fader

MASTERY MAP

★ YOUR GOAL! ★

HOW WILL YOU MEASURE SUCCESS?
Refocus my measurements away from
the number on the scale and toward
my enjoyment of physical activity.
Percent of gym attendance.

FIND YOUR ENJOYMENT

WHO WILL SUPPORT YOU?
My wife and my friend who is also trying to
lose weight. Review this sheet with them monthly.

CHALLENGES?
Sugar cravings; frustrations with not losing
weight "fast enough." Use resetting routine.

HOW WILL YOU GET THERE?
Using FitBit with my wife and friends to have accountability
and healthy competition; being active with my kids; taking
dance classes. Focus on adaptive self-talk mantras.

WHAT IS YOUR PROCESS GOAL?
To make the process of losing weight more enjoyable;
to focus on consistency at the gym.

WHAT IS YOUR MOTIVATION? WHAT IS YOUR POWER VALUE?
To create a healthier lifestyle for myself and reduce my current risk
for developing diabetes, so that I can live longer for my children.

★ WHAT IS YOUR OUTCOME GOAL? ★
Lose 20 pounds.

© Jonathan Fader

ABOUT THE AUTHOR

Jonathan Fader, Ph.D., is the team sport psychologist for Major League Baseball's New York Mets and a Resource Doctor of the MLB rookie program. He is a certified consultant and member of the Association of Applied Sport Psychology. Dr. Fader works with many professional athletes, teams, and other elite performers to improve their performance using proven sport and performance psychology techniques. He consults with a wide array of businesses and organizations on how to improve leadership and performance. Also a licensed clinical psychologist, Dr. Fader is the cofounder of the Union Square Practice, a psychology and psychiatry practice in the heart of New York City.

NOTES

Chapter 1: The Life as Sport Philosophy

1. The quote from poker player Amir Vehdi came from "In Memoriam: Amir Vahedi," WSOP.com, January 11, 2010, www.wsop.com/news/2010/Jan/2656/In-Memoriam-Amir-Vahedi.html.

2. Curtis Granderson's quote about playing for the love of the game came from Steve Kettman, *Baseball Maverick: How Sandy Alderson Revolutionized Baseball and Revived the Mets* (New York: Atlantic Monthly Press, 2015), 241.

3. New research and a summary of previous research on the subject of the amygdala's negative bias can be found in Juraj Kukolja, Thomas E. Schlapfer, Christan Keysers, Deitrich Klingmuller, Wolfgang Meyer, Gereon R. Fink, and Rene Hurlemann, "Modeling a Negative Response Bias in the Human Amygdala by Noradrenergic-Glucocortoid Interactions," *Journal of Neuroscience* 28, no. 48 (November 26, 2008): 12868–12876.

4. The evolution of the human fear response is summarized in H. Stefan Bracha, Adam S. Bracha, Andrew E. Williams, Tyler C. Ralston, and Jennifer Matsukawa, "The Human Fear Circuitry and Fear-Induced Fainting in Healthy Individuals—The Paleolithic-Threat Hypothesis," *Clinical Autonomic Research* 15, no. 3 (June 2015): 238–241.

5. Martin E. P. Seligman's research on survival-related phobias first appeared in "Phobias and Preparedness," *Behavior Therapy* 2, no. 3 (July 1971): 307–320.

6. Research on peak performance for table tennis players was presented by Chang-Yong Chu, Ling-Chung Chen, Chung-Ju Huang, and Tsung-Min Hung, "Sources of Psychological States Related to Peak Performance in Elite Table Tennis Players," 12th ITTF Sports Science Congress, Rotterdam, The Netherlands, May 2011, www.ittf.com/ittf_science/SSCenter/docs/20-62%20Chu%20CY_1.pdf.

7. Drs. Greg Flaxman and Lisa Flook from UCLA provide a comprehensive summary of the current research on mindfulness and present focus at "Brief Summary of Mindfulness Research," http://marc.ucla.edu/workfiles/pdfs/MARC-mindfulness-research -summary.pdf.

Chapter 2: Setting Goals: Building a Mastery Map

1. One of the most influential studies on goals in sports: Judy L. Van Raalte and B. W. Brewer, "Goal Setting in Sport and Exercise," in *Exploring Sport and Exercise Psychology*, 2nd ed., 25–48 (Washington, DC: American Psychological Association, 2001). Other studies include Gary Latham and Edwin Locke, "New Developments in and Directions for Goal-Setting Research," *European Psychologist* 12, no. 4 (January 2007): 290–300; and L. Blaine Kyllo and Daniel M. Landers, "Goal Setting in Sport and Exercise: A Research Synthesis to Resolve the Controversy," *Journal of Sport and Exercise Psychology* 17, no. 2 (1995): 117–137.

2. Paul Lehrer and Richard Gevirtz examine the efficacy of heart rate control through biofeedback in "Heart Rate Variability Biofeedback: How and Why Does It Work?" *Frontiers in Psychology* 5 (July 2014): 756.

3. Gary P. Latham and Edwin A. Locke published another study connecting goals and self-esteem called "Enhancing the Benefits and Overcoming the Pitfalls of Goal Setting," *Organizational Dynamics 35*, no. 4 (2006): 332–340.

4. Latham and Locke also established benchmarks for available and stretch goals in their book *A Theory of Goal Setting and Task Performance* (Englewood Cliffs, NJ: Prentice-Hall, 1990).

5. Maura Scott and Stephen Nowlis expand on the concept of momentum in goal setting in their paper "The Effect of Goal Specificity on Consumer Goal Reengagement," *Journal of Consumer Research* 20, no. 3 (2013): 444–459.

6. Backsliding during habit formation is covered extensively in the seminal work of G. Alan Marlatt and Judith Gordon, *Relapse Prevention: Maintenance Strategies in the Treatment of Addictive Behaviors* (New York: Guilford Press, 1985).

7. "Abstinence Violation Effect" is defined by Susan E. Collins and Katie Witkiewitz in the *Encyclopedia of Behavioral Medicine* (New York: Springer, 2015). An online link to the definition can be found at

"Abstinence Violation Effect," ResearchGate, www.researchgate.net /publication/281298055_Abstinence_violation_effect.

8. Kelly Dwyer summarizes the myths surrounding Michael Jordan's high school basketball career in "Was Michael Jordan Really Cut from his High School Basketball Team?" Yahoo Sports, January 10, 2012, http://sports.yahoo.com/blogs/nba-ball-dont-lie/michael -jordan-really-cut-high-school-team-215707476.html.

9. As quoted in Robert Goldman and Stephen Papson, *Nike Culture: The Sign of the Swoosh* (Thousand Oaks, CA: Sage, 1998), 49.

10. A Dominican University study from 2008 is one of many that establishes the value of writing down goals. See "Dominican Research Cited in Forbes Article," Dominican University, www.dominican. edu/dominicannews/dominican-research-cited-in-forbes-article. Other papers on the subject include those by Sheina Orbell, Sarah Hodgkins, and Paschal Sheeran, "Implementation Intentions and the Theory of Planned Behavior," *Personality and Social Psychology Bulletin* 23, no. 9 (1997): 945–954; and Paschal Sheeran and Sheina Orbell, "Implementation Intentions and Repeated Behaviour: Augmenting the Predictive Validity of the Theory of Planned Behaviour," *European Journal of Social Psychology* 29, no. 2–3 (March–May 1999): 349–369.

Chapter 3: Motivation

1. Various incidents of "hysterical strength" are catalogued and referenced in "Hysterical Strength," Wikipedia, https://en.wikipedia .org/wiki/Hysterical_strength.

2. For a much more in-depth look at the psychophysiological aspect of visualization, consult Tony Morris, Michael Spittle, and Anthony P. Watt, *Imagery in Sport* (Champaign: Human Kinetics, 2005).

3. Jure Robič's story is told in great detail by Daniel Coyle, "That Which Does Not Kill Me Makes Me Stronger," *New York Times*, February 5, 2006, www.nytimes.com/2006/02/05/sports /playmagazine/05robicpm.html?pagewanted=all&_r=0.

4. William Miller and Stephen Rollnick, *Motivational Interviewing: Helping People Change* (New York: Guilford Press, 2012).

5. See D. Markland, R. M. Ryan, V. Tobin, and S. Rollnick, "Motivational Interviewing and Self-Determination Theory," *Journal of Social and Clinical Psychology* 24 (2005): 811–831.

6. Researches Amy Wrzsesniewski, Barry Schwartz, Xiangyu Cong, Michael Kane, Audrey Omar, and Thomas Kolditz established the relative value of internal and external motivation in their study "Multiple Types of Motives Don't Multiply the Motivation of West Point Cadets," *Proceedings of the National Academy of Sciences* 111, no. 30 (July 2014): 10990–10995.

7. Canadian researcher Robert Vallerand established the connection between personal passion and motivation in "Les Passions de l'Ame: On Obsession and Harmonious Passion," *Journal of Personality and Social Psychology* 85, no. 4 (2003): 756–767.

8. Psychologist Ellen Winner talks about the "rage to master" in her book *Gifted Children: Myths and Realities* (New York: Basic Books, 1997).

9. Charles Duhigg's book *The Power of Habit: Why We Do What We Do in Life and Business* expands on the link between behaviors and rewards (New York: Random House, 2014).

10. The story of the Mets' game-by-game MVP awards comes from Mike Puma, "Mets Channeling Their Inner WWE with Postgame Awards Ceremony," *New York Post*, June 17, 2015, http://nypost .com/2015/06/17/mets-channeling-their-inner-wwe-with-postgame -award-ceremony; "The WWE-Style Belt That Every Met Wants to Win," *New York Post*, October 10, 2015, http://nypost.com/2015 /10/10/the-wwe-style-belt-that-every-met-wants-to-win; and "Mets on Cuddyer's Wrestling Belt," MLB.com, October 23, 2015, http://m.mlb.com/video/topic/63106348/v525528883/mets-on -cuddyers-postgame-wrestling-belt-tradition.

11. Deborah Roth Ledley, Brian P. Marx, and Richard Heimberg have published a comprehensive guide to cognitive behavioral therapy called *Making Cognitive-Behavioral Therapy Work:" Clinical Process for New Practitioners*, 2nd ed. (New York: Guilford Press, 2010).

12. University of New Mexico researchers W. R. Miller, J. C'de Baca, D. B. Matthews, and P. L. Wilbourne devised their "Personal Values Card Sort," which was published by the University of New Mexico in 2001, www.motivationalinterviewing.org/sites/default/files /valuescardsort_0.pdf.

13. The website Athletize.com provides a picture gallery of LeBron James's various tattoos, including "Chosen 1" and "No one can see through what I am except for the one who made me."

Chapter 4: Managing Anxiety

1. Kellie Marksberry published an excellent summary of the current research about reducing anxiety through breathing called "Take a Deep Breath," American Institute of Stress, August 10, 2012, www.stress.org/take-a-deep-breath. Also see R. Jerath, m. W. Crawford, V. A. Barnes, and K. Harden, "Self-Regulation of Breathing as a Primary Treatment for Anxiety," *Applied Psychopsychology* 40, no. 2 (June 2015): 107–115.

2. S. Kim, W. T. Roth, and E. Wollburgh, "Effects of Therapeutic Relationship Expectancy, and Credibility in Breathing Therapies for Anxiety," *Bulletin of the Menninger Clinic* 79, no. 2 (2015): 116–130.

3. Psychologists Robert Yerkes and John Dillingham Dodson first published about the relationship between arousal and performance with "The Relation of Strength of Stimulus to Rapidity of Habit-Formation," *Journal of Comparative Neurology and Psychology* 18, no. 5 (November 1908): 459–482. It is one of the most quoted studies in all of psychology.

4. Reggie Jackson's quote about Derek Jeter comes from Glenn Liebman, "5 Great Quotes About Yankees' Derek Jeter," ESPN.com, July 9, 2011, http://espn.go.com/espn/page2/index?id=6752443.

5. Dr. Carol Dweck, *Mindset: The New Psychology of Success* (New York: Random House, 2007). In it she describes the concepts of fixed and growth mind-sets.

6. Drs. Fritz Strack, Leonard Martin, and Sabine Stepper published the results of their pen study in "Inhibiting and Facilitating Conditions of the Human Smile," *Journal of Personality and Social Psychology* 54, no. 5 (May 1988): 768–777.

7. Douglas C. Johnson, Nathaniel J. Thom, Elizabeth A. Stanley, Lori Haase, Alan N. Simmons, Pei-an B. Shih, Wesley K. Thompson, Eric G. Potterat, Thomas R. Minor, and Martin P. Paulus published the results of their study examining the use of breathing techniques and mindfulness training for the treatment of posttraumatic stress disorder in "Modifying Resilience Mechanisms in At-Risk Individuals: A Controlled Study of Mindfulness Training in Marines Preparing for Deployment," *American Journal of Psychiatry* 171, no. 8 (August 2014): (844–853).

Chapter 5: Visualization: Unlock the Power of Your Mind

1. In a study Steven Ungerleider and Jacqueline Golding surveyed more than six hundred Olympic athletes and established a high rate of visualization among them: "Mental Practice Among Olympic Athletes," *Perceptual and Motor Skills* 72, no. 3 (June 1991): 1007–1017. That study is supported and expanded upon by numerous others, like one by Richard Ramsey, Jennifer Cumming, and Martin Gareth Edwards—which showed golfers putted significantly better after using visualization: "Exploring a Modified Conceptualization of Imagery Direction and Golf Putting Performance," *International Journal of Sport & Exercise Psychology* 6, no. 2 (January 2008): 207–223.

2. For a more in-depth look at the psychophysiological aspect of visualization, consult Tony Morris, Michael Spittle, and Anthony P. Watt, *Imagery in Sport* (Champaign: Human Kinetics, 2005).

3. The theories of how neuromuscular patterns are established are discussed in Sheila Jennett, *Dictionary of Sport and Exercise Science and Medicine* (Edinburgh: Churchill Livingstone Elsevier, 2008).

4. The theory of visualization as a kind of psychological exercise and protection against anxiety is discussed in Michael Kent, *Oxford Dictionary of Sports Science and Medicine*, 3rd ed. (Oxford: Oxford University Press, 2006).

Chapter 6: Self-Talk: The Key to Confidence

1. Bill Belichick's assessment of Tom Brady appeared in Bob Socci, "Brady's Vision Unlike Any Other," CBSLocal.com, October 19, 2013.

2. A. T. Beck's 1970 paper, "Cognitive Therapy: Nature and Relation to Behavior Therapy" (*Behavior Therapy* 1, no. 2 [May 1970]: 184–200) was one of the first to fully examine the cognitive aspects of cognitive-behavioral therapy (CBT) techniques.

3. David Barlow and Michelle Craske wrote *Mastery of Your Anxiety and Panic* (Oxford: Oxford University Press, 2006).

4. Napoleon Hill's *Think and Grow Rich* has been published in various editions since 1960. A current one is the paperback version: New York: Tarcher, 2005.

Chapter 7: Set Routines to Win
the Game Before It Begins

1. Dr. Gregg Steinberg describes Jason Day's preshot routine in "The Mental Game: Visualize Results like Day," PGATour.com, February 9, 2015, www.pgatour.com/instruction/2015/02/09/mental -game-visualize-results-jason-day.html.

2. Daniel Gould and Eileen Udry discuss the use of routines to manage arousal in "Psychological Skills for Enhancing Performance: Arousal Regulation Strategies," *Medicine and Science in Sports and Exercise* 26, no. 4 (April 1995): 478–485.

3. Wade Boggs's chicken superstition was covered extensively by John Edward Young in "Chicken Is a Big Hit with Baseball's Wade Boggs," *Christian Science Monitor*, January 2, 1985, www.csmonitor. com/1985/0102/hffoul.html.

4. Serena Williams talked about her superstitions in "Superstitions That Serve Me Well," *Evening Standard*, July 2, 2007, www.standard .co.uk/news/superstitions-that-serve-me-well-by-serena-williams -6594813.html.

5. B. F. Skinner's studies have been widely documented and cited. He wrote about it in his seminal book, *About Behaviorism* (New York: Knopf, 1974).

6. Kolo Touré's late arrival to the second half of a soccer game was recounted in David Hynter, "Superstitious Mind Leaves Toure Red-Faced over his Yellow Card," *Guardian*, February 25, 2009, www.theguardian.com/football/2009/feb/26/champions-league -arsenal-roma. Touré received a yellow card for running out onto the field without the referee's permission.

7. The anecdotes about Stefan Holm are taken from David Epstein, *The Sports Gene: Inside the Science of Extraordinary Performance* (New York: Current, 2014).

8. Matt Duffy's quotes came from his article "The New Kid," *Players Tribune*, September 15, 2015, www.theplayerstribune.com /matt-duffy-giants-the-new-kid.

9. The anecdote about Ken Ravizza using a toilet as a reminder to have a resetting routine comes from Wayne Drehs, "Ravizza Key to Titans' Turnaround," ESPN.com, June 27, 2004, http://espn.go.com/ college-sports/news/story?id=1830586.

Conclusion: Win Today

1. David Wright's quotes come from "The World Series: Memories of Moments to Forget," *New York Times*, November 3, 2015, www.nytimes.com/2015/11/03/sports/baseball/the-world-series-memories-of-moments-to-forget.html.

INDEX